My Father was Carmen Miranda!

Memoirs of an English Showgirl

Memoir of an English Show Girl
© 2008 Nena Jover Kelty. All Rights Reserved.

All illustrations are copyright of their respective owners, and are also reproduced here in the spirit of publicity. Whilst we have made every effort to acknowledge specific credits whenever possible, we apologize for any omissions, and will undertake every effort to make any appropriate changes in future editions of this book if necessary.

No part of this book may be reproduced in any form or by any means, electronic, mechanical, digital, photocopying or recording, except for the inclusion in a review, without permission in writing from the publisher.

Published in the USA by:
BearManor Media
P O Box 71426
Albany, Georgia 31708
www.bearmanormedia.com

ISBN 1-59393-142-5

Printed in the United States of America.

Book and cover design by Darlene and Dan Swanson of Van-garde Imagery, Inc.

Dedication

For all my siblings, and for all the acrobats, dancers, equestrians, and comedians who came before us.

Acknowledgements

To my good friends Julie Beers and Bob Birchard for their constant support and generosity of time with editing and all aspects of what it takes to put a book together. And to my other good friends: Janet Blake, Rosemary Barlow, Juanita Portillo, Mila Paredes Reid, Erika Hansen, Vivian Charlton, Louise and Jack Spillman, and Patrick O'Connor, for their wonderful critiques, encouragement, and support without which this book would never have been possible –all great writers! Thank you all!

Chapter One

The BBC announcer interrupted my favorite music program. "Croydon Aerodrome is under attack!"

I raced up three flights of stairs to the top of the house, flung open a window and looked out toward Croydon only three miles away as the crow flies from Wimbledon. It looked like little toy planes diving over and under each other. They looked so graceful, as if they were in a ballet. I stood transfixed, finding it difficult to grasp that these were not toy planes but a fight to the death between young English and German pilots. Every few minutes a plane fell to the earth in flames. It was a surreal experience made more so by the rare, sunny day. Not a time to die. But dying is a necessary and evil part of war. There would be much more of that before this madness was over. I tore myself away from the window, wishing there were some way to bring back a semblance of normalcy to the world.

It didn't seem possible that my life had changed so drastically in such a short time. Was it really only two years since I was sixteen and answered that ad in the paper: "Wanted: Girl dancers who can swim well." I was on summer break from my all-girl school, could swim and dance, and wanted a job. I grabbed my black tank swimsuit with its "Wimbledon Ladies' Swim Club" badge and headed off to the Underground. The audition was at a pool in the center of London. When I arrived, I saw posters outside for what I thought must be the show I was auditioning for – "England's Water Show of 1939." All the blurbs sounded perfect for a summer job. I walked inside.

Johnny Johnston greeted me with a warm smile and introduced himself. He asked me to do a simple dive and swim a lap. As I pulled myself out of the water, he said, "Great! We leave in two weeks. Next week, you'll go to Jantzen's for swim suits and Max Factor for make-up."

I was flabbergasted, "Does that mean I have the job?"

"Yes, of course."

He didn't even ask me to dance. But he was a diver. I thought someone else might audition me for the dancing part of the job, but no one ever did. I asked Johnny what exactly I'd be doing.

"There'll be six other girls. You'll open the show wearing bathing suits patterned on those of the 1860s over your new Jantzens. You'll rip the old ones off, dive into the pool and do some synchronized swimming. You'll model bathing suits and do a couple of dances. By the way, what kind of dancing can you do?"

"Well, ballet, and I'm a pretty good tap-dancer."

"I don't think any of the other girls can tap-dance. Could you do a solo? I need something to go between the divers and the comedy diving act. You'd have plenty of time to dry off and get ready."

I gulped. Is this for real? Surely this audition isn't the norm? Afraid to let the job get away from me, I nodded and crossed my fingers. My brothers and I had been taking tap-dancing lessons for months from the lead dancer in a London show. I'd have to get busy and put a routine together and decide on some music. A thought occurred to me.

"Where would I dance at a swimming pool?"

"On the side."

"On cement? I'd need a tap mat. Maybe I can borrow my dad's." I was thinking of the one we put down on the concrete floor in the garage when we had our lessons.

"Terrific! By the way, your pay will be five pounds a week."

A fortune! I was ecstatic. I'm actually going to be paid to swim! And my tap lessons are paying off. I thanked Johnny and floated home on a cloud, dying to tell my parents about my new venture.

"But we're going to Germany for the summer!" my mother protested. "Don't you remember? Daddy and Uncle are headlining the bill at the Deutches Theater in Munich. You can't stay in England all by yourself! We'll be gone three months!"

I hadn't forgotten. My dad and his brother, Rafael, were in show business. They did a comedy act called "The Jovers." They'd received an offer for the show and had agreed to take it. Because Germany didn't allow any of its currency to leave the country, Uncle Rafael and my dad decided they'd take their families and spend all the money having a wonderful vacation.

I was determined to join the water show. The excitement of getting my first job was no match for the alternative – spending the summer with my siblings and cousins, all younger than I. My mind was made up, and I was determined not to be swayed.

"I knew you're going to Germany, but I really want this job. I've already agreed to take it."

My fingers were crossed. I know when it came right down to it my parents would have the last word.

"Well, tell us more about it. Who are these people? What will you be doing, and where will you work?"

Well, at least that wasn't a direct "No."

I explained we would tour England and Scotland, performing in outdoor swimming pools. "There'll be three divers – Johnny, Peter Beveridge, the other co-owner, and Buff Orr. There's Larry Griswold, who does a comedy trampoline act, a kayak champion, and we seven girls."

"Yes, but what will you be doing?"

"I'm going to be an aquabelle! I'll do synchronized swimming. We'll perform a hula dance on a grass-covered float in the middle of the pool and another dance where we dress up as penguins. We'll also do some modeling of bathing suits."

And feeling that I was perhaps pushing things a little, I added, "Is it all right if I take the tap mat?"

"What on earth for?"

"Well, when they knew I could tap dance, they asked me to do a solo. I can put the mat down on the side of the pool."

I could see my parents were a little taken aback by this 16-year-old who was suddenly showing independence. I almost screamed for joy when my dad said, "You can take the mat, but I want to come and see your work. I want to meet everybody and see for myself what you're getting into. I'll help you with your solo. We won't make it any longer than two minutes. That's long enough. Always leave them wanting more. Have you thought about what music you'll use? You know, there won't be any musicians. You'll have to get a record that they can play."

Oops! I was so excited that I'd given no thought to mere details. I was grateful for my dad's acceptance of my new venture and his offer to help. I couldn't have had a better mentor. He'd been in show business all his life, starting in Spain in the family circus. His experience and attention to details were invaluable to me.

"What you'll have to look for is a 78-rpm record with an orchestral arrangement with the right tempo, ample introduction time for you to reach the mat, two minutes for the routine, and a finish that ends the same time you do," he said.

It sounded like a big order. For the next two days, I scoured music shops for the perfect record. Big bands were in vogue then, so there were many choices. I finally settled on a jazzy arrangement by Stanley Black of "Tea for Two." It had a nice, lilting beat to it, something I could dance to. The trouble was that it was too long. I'd have to ask someone to pick up the needle after two choruses. In my youthful zeal, I hadn't considered the possibility of human failure in this endeavor. Time would reveal this to be true again and again. With my dad's help, the dance routine went together quickly, and I was ready for my debut.

Next on the agenda was my appointment at Jantzen's, where I met the other girls. All of us were teenagers, and this was the first job for most of us. The Jantzen people told us to select five bathing suits – one for swimming, and the others for modeling. It was exciting to be treated as professionals. They told us we would keep the suits when the show ended. A wardrobe of five bathing suits! What luxury!

"And here are your bathing hats," the instructor said.

They were really chic – white with a little embossed pattern, and no strap. We loved the snug fit and modern look.

From there, we traipsed over to Max Factor where the instructors showed us how to apply the new pancake make-up: dipping the sponge in water, rubbing it on this cake, then dabbing it on our faces. It was a very pale color. It took ages to put on, and I was not happy with the result. My face was now several shades lighter than the rest of my tanned skin, my cheeks were rosy red, and the mascara made my eyes itch. The instructor, who'd obviously not listened when told what we would be doing, warned us not to get the mascara wet! It was not waterproof. I looked around at the other girls. We all looked like painted dolls.

When the session was over, we thanked the ladies, picked up our bathing suits and bags of make-up, and went for a cup of tea. It was our first opportunity to get acquainted.

"How did you like the make-up?" I asked the girls as soon as we were settled.

"I didn't," they chorused.

I was relieved. Mary spoke up, "It's okay for the theatre, but it's wrong for a swimming pool. I think I'll just use some lipstick."

"Great idea. I'll do the same."

Even though it seemed the make-up session had been a waste of time, we had to admit we loved all the attention. After we introduced ourselves, I learned that only two of us had any professional background in dancing: Betty was a ballerina, and Mary had been a chorus girl in a West End production. It was she who taught us the hula dance and a funny eccentric routine for when we wore our penguin costumes. Toni was a good swimmer, and Lynette, Helen and Tiny had attended dance schools but had no professional experience.

After two weeks of intensive rehearsals, we aquabelles knew our routines, the other members of the show had gathered, and we were ready for our opening. It went well. Nothing disastrous happened, and we were all excited over our participation in a new venture.

As it happened, my dad was working at Chiswick Empire Theatre, so it was easy for him and my mother to come and see the show in Wood Green. They enjoyed it, liked everyone in it, and approved of my participation. Although proud of my initiative, they were uneasy about letting their 16-year-old daughter go off on her own while they were in Germany. The day after they gave their okay, my mother said, "Daddy wants to talk to you."

Uh-oh.

He took me to the drawing room, shut the door and told me to sit down. Here come the birds and bees, I thought, and wondered how he would approach it. He paced back and forth, not saying a word. Suddenly, he stopped in front of me and blurted out, "If a man says to you 'You're beautiful!' don't pay any attention." And with that he fled the room. I sat there stunned. That's it? No birds and bees? Evidently not. That episode was the extent of my sex education as far as my parents were concerned.

Our next performance was to be outside London, and as the family was leaving soon for Germany, we said our goodbyes and made promises to write. With a "See you in September!" they left.

Chapter Two

I loved everything about the water show – the chance to swim every day, the traveling, and the camaraderie of young people. We performed in every kind of weather. Sometimes it was hard to smile as we came up after a dive into freezing water. But there was one pool where we enjoyed the unusual luxury of heated sea water. It was in Bournemouth on the south coast, a haven for mostly retired, rich people.

It never occurred to any of us to miss a performance when it was our "time of the month." Mary told us about Tampax which worked long enough for a quick dash to the pool, a two-minute swim, then back to the dressing room where we could change again. The dunking in cold water seemed to shut down our systems temporarily, which also helped. Our dressing rooms were unheated cement cubicles, but we were young, this was England after all, and none of us expected to be comfortable all the time. My solo went well, but I was glad my dad couldn't see the water being splashed onto his tap mat. It'll be a wreck by the end of the tour, I thought.

We girls were earning enough to stay in hotels and never bothered to book ahead. We bunked together in twos, threes and fours, whatever worked out best. I didn't need to spend money on clothes or entertainment and was with a great group of people. I never wanted it to end.

The family sent me postcards telling of the wonderful time they were having in Munich. The show was a big success. Adolph Hitler even attended one night with his posse of SS guards. Apparently, he had a special interest in that theatre, having paid out of his own pocket for its restoration. The family was staying in a house they rented at Starnberger See, a lake just outside the city. They went swimming every day and took boats out on the lake. It sounded like they were all enjoying themselves. There was never a word about the political situation and how they felt about it. However, I was nervous and wondered if they were getting the same news we were.

Every day brought reports of what Hitler was doing, and everyone wondered how far he would go before the British Government felt compelled to act. Neville Chamberlain's efforts to appease Hitler were fruitless, and war seemed inevitable. England made some steps to prepare for a possible invasion; at seaside resorts, rolls of barbed wire were strung along the beaches, and everyone was issued a gas mask with instructions to have it on his person at all times. Road signs were removed. If the enemy ever made it over here, he could jolly well find his own way around.

To my great relief, one day in the middle of August, my dad telephoned to tell me they were all safely back in Wimbledon. I couldn't wait to see them but still had a couple of weeks to go on my contract. It was a shock to learn that my aunt, uncle and cousins were not returning to England. I'd have to wait until I got home to hear the whole story.

Then, on September 3, 1939, while we were performing in Hastings on the south coast, Germany invaded Poland. England had no choice but to honor its treaty with Poland and declare war on Germany. A few minutes later, air raid sirens went off. I was in the pool at the time, enjoying it all to myself. I thought, "Oh no, Field Marshall Hermann Goering and his Luftwaffe are here already. He's going to bomb us out of existence, just like he threatens." I scrambled out of the pool, dressed quickly and grabbed my gas mask. Turning on the radio, I learned that the air raid warning was a false alarm – the airplane crossing the English coastline was one of ours. I sighed with relief, having been so sure that my end had come. The calm voice of the BBC announcer reassured his audience that no Germany planes were in sight.

With the announcement of war, the show fell apart. The Americans and Canadians were anxious to go home while transportation was still available. We drove in a long caravan of cars to London where we would go our separate ways. As Wimbledon was on the way, we stopped at my home where my mother served tea and cake to everyone. My dad apologized for the meager servings. They had not expected 15 drop-in guests. He shrugged and said with a grin, "There's a war on."

After everyone left, my dad was very quiet, not his usual buoyant self. He didn't seem to want to talk about his time in Munich other than to say that his brother, Rafael, was not returning to England. I was shocked. Auntie Margarita, who was German, was afraid of being interned if they came back to England.

"What will happen to their beautiful home in Worcester Park?" I said.

"I don't know. Your uncle still has his Swiss passport, so they'll spend the war in Switzerland. They'll be OK."

"I went with Daddy to the British Embassy!" my little sister, Fe, blurted out.

"What was that all about?" I asked my dad.

He told me the whole story. A letter arrived summoning him to the embassy, where the consul strongly urged him to return to England immediately. War with Germany was imminent. My dad assured the consul he would leave as soon as possible. As they started toward the door, they could hear two women talking in another room. In a shrill voice, one asked, "Is there going to be a war?"

"Darn!" the consul said. "That's Unity Mitford, Hitler's friend. I'm not going to tell her anything. Thank you for coming, and good luck!"

With that he quickly shut the door, and my dad and sister Fe went on their way. As they left, they took a quick glance at this notorious lady, considered a traitor by many of her countrymen.

With his brother's blessing, my dad went to the manager of the theatre to ask for release from their contract. The manager refused. He said, "Without your act, I have no show. Anyway, England will never go to war against Germany!"

My dad believed otherwise and was determined to leave. He secretly started to plan. His biggest problem was getting enough petrol for the car to reach the Swiss border. It was in short supply. The routine was that as you pulled into the petrol station, the attendant looked at your gas gauge. If it was low, you could buy a couple of liters. After getting his precious two liters, my dad went back to the house, siphoned the petrol out of the tank into a milk bottle, stuck it under the bed, and then went back to a different station to repeat the process. Finally, after a couple of days, he had enough to fill the tank. He told his brother, and they did the act that night as if nothing was unusual. Afterwards, Rafael helped my dad remove some of his props and precious concertina from the theatre by lowering them out of a window to his waiting car.

My mother had all the kids dressed in warm clothes. All that was left to do was say their goodbyes. At this point, my dad suddenly stopped talking. He couldn't continue.

"Daddy cried," said Fe in a sad little voice.

I could just imagine what an emotional moment that must have been. The two brothers didn't know if they'd ever see each other again. After a couple of minutes, my dad was able to continue with his story. He said that Rafael urged him to leave before the theatre manager could learn of what was happening. My parents, brothers and sister climbed into the car and drove away. They reached the Swiss border, refilled the tank and started their race to Calais, France, to catch the boat to England. As they drove through towns, people shouted for them to douse their lights. It was harrowing driving fast without lights, but they finally reached Calais where they were dismayed to discover a long line of cars ahead of them.

My dad was faced with another problem when he went to buy the tickets: German Marks were the last currency the ticket man wanted to see. A Good Samaritan, overhearing my dad's problem, came to the rescue and paid the fares for the whole family and the car for the boat ride to England.

"Things will be very different for us now, Nena," he said. "You and the boys won't be able to go back to your schools. We can't afford them anymore. I'll have to get some kind of job."

I felt sorry for my dad. It must have been a wrenching experience leaving his brother in Germany. They had been together ever since my dad was born, working in some of the most prestigious theatres all over the world. They'd appeared in Royal Command Performances and were highly respected in their profession. What on earth would he do now? The political situation didn't help. Memories of World War I were still strong in the minds of all European countries. They didn't want to get involved, but even if it had to go it alone England was determined to resist the Nazis, no matter the cost. The government constantly warned us that we would have to tighten our belts, that huge sacrifices were ahead for everybody. Jobs were scarce, and many factories closed down. The present was grim, but the future looked even grimmer.

Wanting to help out, I started scouring the want-ads for work. The first one I answered was for a music copier, but I was too late – the job was already taken. The next was for an ambulance assistant. I applied at the local fire station. The fireman who interviewed me could hardly contain his scorn as he looked me up and down.

"Could you pick up a body whose head has been blown off? Could you pick up body parts and put them in a bag?" he asked.

Before he could ask me another question, I murmured, "No," and fled. What was I thinking – me, who can't stand the sight of blood. I crept home holding my side which suddenly started to hurt. I tried to ignore it, thinking my failure to find a job had something to do with it.

However, that evening the pain persisted, and my dad, convinced I was making too much fuss, said, "You're giving into it. Come here! Let me rub it."

He rubbed my stomach vigorously, and I promptly fainted. The doctor was called, and I was rushed to hospital where they removed my appendix. After a week there, it was good to come home. My mother, six months pregnant, already had her hands full: there were my three brothers, my sister, my dad and my grandmother, Virginia Jover. Now there was me recovering from surgery.

However, we did have a live-in helper. My mother met Berry, a nurse, when she had visited the hospital years ago. We treated her as one of the family. She had been raised in an orphanage and had had a rough life.

I was in bed one evening when I heard a commotion downstairs. My mother was shouting, "Mama! Wake up! Mama! Are you all right?"

I rushed downstairs to find my mother bent over Mama Jover, who was lying on the floor, muttering incoherently.

"What happened? What's the matter with her?"

"I don't know. I found her like this. Berry's away for the weekend. Stay with her while I fetch Grandma Andrews next door. She used to be a nurse. Maybe she'll know what to do. I've already called the doctor."

By now, the rest of the family had gathered around gaping, not sure what to do. Mama Jover was now snoring quietly, oblivious to us all. Soon, Mrs. Andrews, a very kind and motherly lady, arrived. She took one look at Mama, turned to my mother and in a most genteel voice said, "My dear, she's drunk!"

All we kids burst out laughing, but my mother was livid.

"How could this be?" she wanted to know. "There's no liquor in the house."

At that moment, the doorbell rang, and my mother rushed to answer, anxious to escape the embarrassment. She still had a faint hope that Mama wasn't really drunk but had some minor thing wrong with her. It was the doctor. He examined Mama, who was still on the floor, and agreed with Mrs. Andrews' diagnosis.

"Yes, she's found a little cheer somewhere. How old is the lady?"

"She's eighty-five."

"My! She's sturdy for her age."

He put his stethoscope away and said, "Just put her to bed. She'll be all right in the morning." He patted my mother on the shoulder and said, "Don't worry. She's a strong lady."

We all helped carry Grandmother to bed. It was not easy as we had to go up two flights of stairs, and she was dead weight. To add to our problems, her arms were flopping around, and her head kept bobbing up and down. We had to stop several times to put her arms back on her stomach and hold her head up. To make matters even worse, she kept repeating, "Kiss me, man! Kiss me, man!"

This sent us into fits of giggles, and it was all we could do to hang on to her. We finally got her to bed, took off her shoes and covered her with a blanket.

"I'd like to know whatever it was she drank," said Mummy.

The mystery of Grandmother's inebriation was solved when it was time for me to have my daily glass of Wincarnis – a tonic wine the doctor had prescribed for me after surgery. The bottle was almost empty!

"From now on, lock it up in your wardrobe," said Mummy.

Chapter Three

Mama Jover was not your average, sweet little grandmother who sat in the corner crocheting. Although we kids thought she was funny, she was a trial to the adults with her shenanigans. In the past, they would pass her back and forth between the two families. Now, there was only our family. We had to learn how to cope with her full time.

My dad missed all the problems Grandmother caused as he was at work. A friend got him a job delivering bolts of fabric to factories. That dried up quickly when clothes rationing started and factories converted to make army uniforms. Yardage was now delivered by the truck load. Then a friend told him about a milkman's job. So, my dad would get up at 5:00 a.m. and drive to the other side of London to get the milk. Then he had to deliver it. Not knowing all the streets on his route, it took him forever. He would drag himself home late in the evening, eat a quick dinner, fall into bed, then get up a few hours later to repeat the routine all over again. He was not too proud to do these menial jobs, but despite his hard work he was not earning very much money.

It was a sad time, not only for my family but for the whole country. As we listened to the BBC news, our hearts sank. France had already fallen, and Holland, Belgium and Norway quickly followed and surrendered to the German Wehrmacht. It was a sobering thought – Britain was now the only country left taking a stand against Hitler. We were unprepared for this challenge or the subsequent tragedy of Dunkirk when British troops were driven out of France by the advancing Germans. They left behind precious guns, ammunition and tanks. We were also short of planes and trained pilots. Our situation seemed hopeless, but I never heard one person say we should give up.

Matters came to a head when the British Parliament finally decided that Prime Minister Neville Chamberlain had to go. His half-hearted conduct of the war provoked a vote of censure. Labor and Liberals refused to serve under him, and even a member of his own party invoked the words of Oliver Cromwell as he said to him, "Depart, I say, and let us have with you. In the name of God, go!"

A new Prime Minister, Winston Churchill, was elected, and when he gave his "We will never surrender" speech, he spoke for all of us. We were behind him 100%, even though all he could offer his country was "blood, toil, tears and sweat."

As my dad was trying to fulfill his responsibilities as a milkman, air-raids were disrupting his route. Sometimes he found that houses he had to deliver to had been bombed, and many of the streets he had to drive down were full of craters. He looked depressed and discouraged.

Chapter Four

One Sunday morning in the fall of '39, we were all having breakfast together when my dad looked at Raf and me and said, "I want to talk to both of you."

"What have we done wrong?" I wondered.

He got right to the point.

"I'm going back into show business. I don't like these jobs I've been doing, and I can't make enough money to support the family. You're going to have to work with me in an act. Let's go in the other room. Show me what you can do!"

Oh, no! Audition for my dad? What will he think of my small repertoire? It was true I had worked in the water show for three months and the year before had even danced in the chorus line of a pantomime my dad was appearing in, but this was different. The thought of working side-by-side with such a seasoned performer was intimidating. But, then, I thought about my vulnerable position with the government – too old for regular government schools (17) and too young for most jobs. I had no skills anyway and would be assigned to a munitions factory before too long. Raf was in the same position. It seemed we had no choice. As the French would say, "C'est la guerre!"

Raf and I looked at each other and shrugged.

"You go first," he said.

I sat down at the piano and played, "Autumne" by Chaminade, a piece with lots of runs and variations.

"Er, don't you know something more, um, modern?"

"No, 'fraid not. All I have is classical music. But I can learn something else. I'll go to the music shop and see what they have."

"Okay. Pick something you can get away with in Wigan. Remember, we won't be playing the Albert Hall. What else can you do?"

"Well, there's that tap dance I did in the water show ...."

"I may have Raf do that. Raf, can you play anything on that guitar of yours?"

"I can't play a solo, but I'm not bad otherwise."

"Well, let me hear something."

Raf was mostly self-taught, but he was musical and had a good ear. Later, when he was in the Royal Marines, he became a member of their "Marineers Band," the first jazz band of the corps. He played a few riffs and chords. It sounded good to me.

At the end of our auditions, we looked at Daddy in apprehension. His face was grim, but he managed a strangled, "Good. Let's get to work."

I prayed I was up to the task. My dad's rich theatrical background was awesome. Florencio Tomas Jover was born in Spain where his grandparents owned a circus. His mother, Virginia, one of their daughters, was a fine equestrian who trained her own ponies for her bareback riding act. She was a widow at thirty-three with three young sons when she met Julian Jover, my dad's father. They fell in love and got married. Julian was only twenty-three. He had been only eighteen when the circus arrived in Madrid and he left home to join their acrobatic team.

Julian taught acrobatics to his stepsons and son Tommy, eventually forming an act with them. For several years they toured throughout Europe and in 1914 moved to England when Henry Sherek, an English agent on a talent search, signed them up for an extensive tour. Shortly after arriving, the family experienced a tragic loss – Lorenzo died of a massive heart attack. Julian, taking the event hard, decided to retire. This created a crisis – there was no way they could continue doing this complicated acrobatic act with three people.

Carlos and Rafael were in their early thirties, getting near retirement age for acrobats, and Tommy, ten years younger, was ready for a big change. They got together and agreed to form a comedy act. Tommy had always envied comedians who strolled onto the stage, told a few jokes, then strolled off. They didn't have to lug all that heavy equipment from city to city, erect it, and pull it down. And they didn't have to go on last in every show. The brothers got together and, using all their experience from years in the circus, created their comedy act which they called "The Three Jovers." The act was an immediate success, and they had no trouble getting work.

One night tragedy struck again when Carlos was doing the feet-to-feet trick that was the big finish to the act, he fell, hitting his head badly. He was unable to continue, and the manager dropped the curtain. The injuries that Carlos sustained were serious and despite all the efforts from doctors he was unable to recover and died. The two brothers were devastated but there was little time to mourn. They were supporting ever growing families. The new act they formed was even more successful than the previous. For fifteen years they worked all over the world in the most prestigious theatres and performed in Royal Command Performances. Knowing all this, I couldn't help but be intimidated. I was in awe of all my dad's accomplishments.

For the next few weeks, Dad gave us a crash course in show business. We practiced how to get on and off the stage gracefully and project our voices as we delivered lines. He taught us a few tango steps, and I spent hours at the music shop searching for something more appropriate than "Chaminade." Then he thought of something else he'd like me to do. Carmen Miranda was very popular at the time, and I should do an impersonation of her. By now, I was getting excited over the whole idea, and thought, "Why not?" My mother showed me how to make a headdress using buckram, a stiff material. Instead of covering it with fruit as Carmen did, I'd have to be content with ostrich feathers and flowers.

As Dad explained, the curtain goes up with me at the piano. I needed something dramatic and finally settled on George Gershwin's "Rhapsody in Blue." I loved that music the first time I heard it. Why does it sound so American, I wondered, and how did the composer dream up that sound? I'd have to memorize it. I always felt more secure with music in front of me, but in showbiz that's a big no-no. At least, I only had to play 16 bars. The last thing Raf and I learned was how to take a bow. We fervently hoped there'd be a need for that skill.

My dad worked out a rough outline for a 15-minute act. Following the introduction, I get up from the piano, pick up a violin and walk down stage. I have to be careful how I handle the instrument as it is a prop, and I must avoid the embarrassment of its premature collapse. I stand ready with bow poised, ready to "perform" a solo, when my dad comes on and interrupts me. Each time I'm about to start "playing," he interrupts me again until finally he asks me, "Do you mind if I smoke?"

Thoroughly exasperated, I answer, "I don't care if you burn!"

With that, he reaches into his pocket, pulls out a huge prop cut-throat razor and slices my violin in half. I look in dismay at my instrument, glare in disgust at him, then storm off the stage.

At this point, Raf comes on with his guitar. They both sit down. My dad picks up his concertina, which had been placed next to their two chairs, and they start playing, interrupting each other once in a while with a joke. After about five minutes of this, and to the confusion of both, I make a sudden entrance and do my impersonation of Carmen Miranda, singing, "I, yi, yi, yi, I like you very much." Then I exit, and my dad follows me. This is where Raf does his tap dance. When he finishes, I come on again dressed in a Spanish costume. Raf and I start to dance a tango. My dad returns dressed as a woman and not just any woman but a real floozy with pipe-cleaner eyelashes, a veil, huge earrings and wearing a two-piece dress with a bare midriff – a garish version of my outfit. He lures Raf away from me, and they do a very funny burlesque tango, ending with my dad going headfirst with a loud bang into a guitar – another prop. The act ends with my dad sitting on the floor, the guitar hanging around his neck. The curtain comes down, and we take our curtain calls.

The burlesque tango was something he used to do with his brother, but this time he took the female part. The act had some things going for it – lots of experience and a good sense of comedy from my dad, and two young people. My 16-year-old brother was tall, dark and handsome – a rarity in any act during the war – and I felt comfortable with what I was doing.

My dad made both of the musical props. He started with real instruments, carefully sawing around the edges and cutting the parts into smaller pieces. He strengthened the backs of these pieces, then sanded them. After that, he glued a piece of string to each loose part and fastened the other end to the inside of the body of the instrument. When this was done, he put all the pieces together. The result was a very convincing musical instrument, although of course you could never play it. The beauty of this design was that we could pick up each instrument after it was broken and never worry about losing a piece. The string took care of that. My dad added an extra feature to the guitar. The force of impact triggered explosives embedded in small corks, which had been made to order at a fireworks factory. That extra bang added to the dramatic effect of the trick. Before each performance, I put my violin together, and Raf assembled the cello. Both violin and cello lasted for years and never needed repairs.

Chapter Five

In November 1939, my dad decided the act was ready. He visited agents who in the past had fallen over themselves to book him and his brother. But things were different now. "Where can I see you work?" they wanted to know. At last, we got a date in Chesterfield, an industrial city in the Midlands, not exactly a number one date. But it was a start, a place where we could knock the rough edges off our performances and find out what worked and what didn't. Raf and I were more than nervous. I was petrified. Being all alone on the stage for the first minute of the act made me appreciate what pressures a stand-up comedian goes through. Somehow, we got through the first performance without missing any cues. After the show, my dad seemed pleased. Perhaps it was due to the fact he was back in familiar surroundings, doing what he did best. But maybe he also saw some potential in both of us. He said, "You both did well. There are just a couple of little things we need to work on, nothing major."

That was welcome praise indeed. The next show found us more relaxed.

We learned later that the man who booked us thought he was getting "The Two Jovers," not "Tommy Jover with Nena and Raf."

"You have a nerve thinking you could get that act for what you're paying us," said my dad. But at least the ice was broken, the word got around, and we began to get work. One early criticism was that "Nena looks like a school girl." They got that right. Just six months before I had been wearing black wool stockings and a navy blue tunic which had to be four inches above the knee when kneeling – part of my school dress code. My parents decided something had to be done to make me look older and more sophisticated. They'd start with my dresses which they realized were too girlish.

Clothes were rationed, and people in show business didn't get any special consideration. It would not be easy to find what I needed, and, besides, there was little money to pay for anything elaborate. Mummy mentioned our dilemma to her cousin who owned a dry-cleaning shop. Emma said she had several unclaimed dresses we could have. Their owners had never come to collect them. With a war on, there was no place to wear such fancy clothes, and they didn't want to pay the dry-cleaning bill. They'd been worn only once, when their owners were presented at court. The material was of very high quality – beautiful satins and velvets. All the dresses had long trains. Emma gave them to us with her blessings. Mummy was very resourceful and sewed beautifully. She picked the dresses apart and made lovely costumes out of them for me – far nicer than anything we could have bought.

Wearing these creations made me feel beautiful, but there was a side effect for which I was not prepared – sudden attention from the opposite sex. I thought they had all gone mad. My sheltered life did not prepare me for this. I didn't know how to banter or laugh off crude remarks. Until I matured a little, I didn't handle it well, greeting any advance with a rude remark. Most of the men were older. I longed to meet a young man who would like to play tennis, go swimming or was interested in music. But, alas, they were all in the services.

Even if I'd met such a young man at that time in my life, I probably wouldn't have handled that well either. Every time a man even looked at me, my mother's words of warning rang in my ear. It was hard to reconcile the alluring and sexy dresses she made for me with the dire words of warning about men she kept repeating. It was confusing. My mind kept going back to my mother's reaction on that day when a boy first showed any interest in me.

I was 16, attending a presentation of Handel's "Messiah" which my school put on every year. It was open to the public. After it was over, a boy I'd never met came up to me and asked if he could walk me home. He said he went to the same school as my brothers and knew them. I saw no harm in it. As we strolled along, we talked about the sports we liked and the latest pictures. He was good company. When we arrived at my house, my mother was leaning out the window with a grim look on her face. She was waiting for me. Knowing how she felt about consorting with the opposite sex, I thought to myself, "I'd better do this right." I introduced Buzz and told her that he asked to walk me home. She put her lips in a thin line and just nodded her head. Recognizing a storm signal when I see one, I quickly thanked Buzz, said, "Goodnight," and went into the house.

My mother stood there with her arms folded.

"Well! I thought you were different!" she said.

"What do you mean? I haven't done anything. He just walked me home."

"Well, I've told you enough times how men are. One thing leads to another, and they're all after the same thing. Don't let me see you with that boy again!"

I was crushed. This was so unfair. It wasn't that I had any feelings for Buzz, whom I'd only just met, but hopes for any future relationship with the opposite sex looked dismal. As it happened, although I was intimidated by my mother, Buzz wasn't. He found out that I rode my bike to school every day and had to cross Mitcham Common. I was halfway across one day when there he was, waiting beside the path. I got off my bike, and we stood there for a few minutes talking. This happened several times before my mother found out. You'd have thought I'd committed a cardinal sin. She accused me of meeting him in all sorts of places I'd never even been. I decided that this liaison, such as it was, wasn't worth all the aggravation. The next time I saw him, I told Buzz we couldn't meet again. He didn't say anything but handed me a note. I took it, then rode off to school. During recess, after reading it, I tore it up into tiny little pieces and stuffed them in my blazer pocket.

The next day was Saturday, and being on the school netball team I had a match to play. I left the house early in the morning and got back at lunchtime. My mother met me at the door with a triumphant look on her face.

"I want you to see something," she said. I followed her to my bedroom, and when she pointed to my bed I couldn't believe my eyes. There was my note from Buzz, all dozens of pieces of it patched together. She must have spent all morning doing it. But why was she so pleased with herself? All it said was, "We're not doing anything wrong. Why won't your mother let us meet?"

"I told you not to see that boy again!" she said.

"He just gave me the note! That's all. We're not meeting anywhere!"

All this aggravation was too much for me, but Buzz was tenacious. He came around to visit my mother. I never knew what was said and wasn't that interested, but the result was my mother made a complete turnaround. Buzz was now the golden boy, welcome at our house any time. He was there for lunch, and he was there for tea, often.

One day, Buzz came around driving his father's car and asked if he could take me for a ride. My mother said, "Yes," but felt compelled to come up with some sort of insurance against the possible loss of her daughter's virginity. She insisted we take with us my little two-year-old brother, Richard. I sat him on my lap, and we took off. I enjoyed several jaunts into the countryside with Buzz until the day Richard, unable to hold himself any longer, wee-ed right in my lap. I was so embarrassed and tried to hide the big stain on my skirt as I ran into the house. Neither

Buzz nor I ever said a word about it, and I never drove into the country with him again.

After I went into show business and we were traveling all the time, Buzz and I didn't keep in touch with each other, although I heard that my mother frequently invited him over for a meal.

Chapter Six

As we worked around England and Scotland in different theatres and shows, we had to make small adjustments to the act. Most of them concerned music. The problems came to light at band rehearsal. On one occasion, an organist asked if I would mind not playing "Rhapsody in Blue." He used it to open his act, claiming Gershwin had personally given him permission to use it as his signature tune. My first reaction was that he didn't have any more right to use that music than I did. Why should I be the one to change? But he was polite, and as music was his whole act, I didn't want to mess it up. I agreed not to play it, giving no thought to the ramifications of my decision.

"Why did you do that?" said my dad. "He can't claim ownership to that music. Now what are you going to do? We don't have anything else for that spot."

"I'm sorry, but what could I do? He was so nice about it. Anyway, the audience doesn't want to hear the same music twice, even if we are in different acts. What if I play Liszt's 'Hungarian Rhapsodie #2'? I can remember 16 bars of that."

"That's classical music. Remember, we're in Morecombe. I wish you hadn't gotten us into this mess."

"But I know that music by heart. I think it will work. It starts with all those big chords."

"Well, you'd better know what you're doing. Tell you what, if you can go out and get me a copy of that music, I'll try to get someone to write parts for the orchestra in time for the show tonight."

Grateful that he didn't get really angry with me, I dashed out and within an hour was back at the theatre with a whole book of Liszt's Rhapsodies. My dad had managed to get the pianist to agree to write the parts for all six musicians – the typical size for a wartime pit orchestra. There was no time for rehearsal.

As the curtain rose, I played the first few bars, praying the musicians would keep in tempo with me. I wanted to cross my fingers but needed them for the big chords. The 16 bars went by smoothly, and the crisis was over. After the act, my dad made me promise I'd never make a decision like that again without asking him first.

We had to change another piece of music every time we worked on the bill with the popular singer Vera Lynn. Her signature tune was "Wishing," the music Raf used for his tap dance. When a big star asks you not to use a certain piece of music (in this case, her manager did the asking), you don't argue. Raf substituted "I Want to be Happy" for "Wishing," making everyone happy. Although we worked with Vera Lynn several times, we never met her. It wasn't that she was a snobbish star who didn't want to mix with the rest of the show; she was simply a very shy person.

I had to make another change when our agent booked us into a traveling revue called *Shoot the Works*. The producer did not want us to open the act with the piano.

"There's not enough time to set it up," he said. "I have a cabaret scene in the second half. I want you to play a piano solo there instead."

I was not excited about this, but as usual my dad had an idea.

"There are too many piano solos around. We'll have to make yours different somehow. How about a solo with the left hand only?"

I'd never heard of such a thing, but my music teacher told me about

Scriabine, a Finnish composer who had written a piece for the left hand. I got the music, but it was not suitable for English Music Halls. I'd have to find something else.

A solution quickly arrived. There was a band in the show, and my dad asked one of the musicians to write something for me. He came up with a great arrangement of "Indian Love Call." I really liked it, and with only one hand to worry about, memorized it easily. Fired up by this success, my dad had another idea that he thought would enhance my solo.

"You know what would be great, Nena. If you held a long cigarette holder in your right hand and took a puff every once in a while."

"Oh, no, I can't do that!" I protested. "I have enough to think about playing the piano without taking up smoking. I'd probably have a coughing fit. And as for a cigarette holder...."

I was so adamant that he quickly gave in. He probably thought there's only so much a 17-year-old can do to look sophisticated. The left-hand solo turned out to be a good move. When we appeared on the same bill as serious pianists, it didn't look like I was trying to compete. But it did mystify them. One day, Rawicz, of the famous duo of Rawicz and Landauer who played on two pianos in their act, asked me, "Why do you play the piano with only one hand when you can play so much better with two?"

I just shrugged. How would he know what it was like for a young girl, playing with one hand or even two, to follow two pianists of their caliber? He'd probably never been that terrified.

We started working for ENSA (Entertainment National Service Association) which was an organization created by the government for the purpose of providing entertainment for men and women in the armed services. Every young person in the country who was not in school was required to do some sort of national service to help the war effort. Those in show business had to give at least six weeks per year to entertaining troops. Although the pay was low, ENSA was a boon to our act. It gave Raf and me much needed experience and a chance to hone our skills.

We worked at several army bases around London and even managed to book a few dates in real theatres. Christmas 1939 saw us in Belfast, Ireland, and New Year's Eve in Limerick. My mother was expecting her baby at the end of January, so we hoped we would be back in time for the big event. I wondered how many times my dad had been gone when my mother was giving birth to the rest of us. We boarded the ferry in Liverpool. The officer checking passports let Raf and me through, but told my dad to step aside. Raf and I watched from the boat as they questioned him for half an hour. Finally, he was allowed to board.

"What was that all about?" we wanted to know.

"Well, my passport is covered with swastika stamps, and they wanted to know why I had gone to Germany so many times. You know how it is with all the rumors about Ireland being a hot-bed of spies. You can't blame the government for being super cautious."

On our dates in Ireland, we worked with Phyllis Dixey who did a striptease act. We became very friendly with her and her husband, going on long walks in the beautiful Irish countryside. We worked on the same bill several times. Phyllis was always careful about having other girls in the same show as her. I was acceptable because I was a brunette. She wanted to be the only blonde in the show.

Later, Phyllis was featured in the *Whitehall Follies* at the Whitehall Theatre in London. In her act, she carried on a comic dialog as she stripped. It was only at the end of her act that she bared all – to thunderous applause.

After Ireland, we got more work with ENSA. For three weeks, it was around London. The last week, when we were working at the big army base in Aldershot, my sister Juanita was born. A friend of ours drove my mother to the hospital. It was a trying experience for my mother as she was all alone through delivery and afterward. Air raid sirens were going off, quickly followed by bombs dropping. We dashed home as quickly as possible. When she was older, Juanita was grateful that our mother had not saddled her with the name "Sireenee," the fate of many unfortunate girls born during an air raid.

Working so close to home, we were only gone a few hours each day and were able to help run the house and look after the younger siblings while my mother recuperated.

Chapter Seven

In the middle of February 1940, ENSA phoned and asked my dad to come in for an interview. This was unusual, and we all wondered what it was about. We found out at tea time when he burst through the door and announced, "We're going to France with ENSA for a month!"

"How can you go to France?" Mummy asked. "We're at war!"

"They asked for volunteers. We'll get extra money because of the danger."

"Well, just how dangerous will it be?"

"Not very. We're going to be sworn in to the BEF (British Expeditionary Force) so if the Germans capture us, we won't be shot as spies. There's nothing to worry about."

I could see my mother was not that reassured. "Well, tell us more. The extra money would be nice, but if you might get killed it's not worth the risk."

"Well, will it make you feel better if I told you that George Formby is heading the show? I'm sure ENSA wouldn't put a big star like him in any danger."

"George Formby! Well, that's different. It must be all right, but a month's a long time."

I felt sorry for my mother. It suddenly hit me that her whole married

43

life had been one long series of partings. Now she was 40 years old, had three young children, including a tiny baby, to look after. When we older ones were small, until we reached school age, she had always traveled with my dad. On each trip, they took one of us with them and left the others with various relatives. Sometimes they'd be gone for six months or more. But there came a time when my mother had to decide whether we would be a band of gypsies forever roaming the earth or settle down and be a more or less normal family. Lucky for all of us, she decided to be a stay-at-home mother and send us off to school. The closest she ever came to complaining of her lot in life was the day she confided in me about what she would have done if she hadn't had children – run a little shop selling yarn. It didn't sound too exciting to me.

Before Raf and I could be inducted into the BEF, for some reason I, being female, had to be interviewed by the police. I was summoned to the historical police station, The Old Bailey. My mouth dropped open when a lady, resplendent in a navy blue uniform, walked toward me. She looked smart and efficient. I had no idea there were women in the police force – and a sergeant at that! She smiled and asked me a few questions. I was so in awe of her that I could hardly utter anything intelligent. Apparently it was enough to convince her I was no threat to the army, for she told me to place my hand on a Bible and then swore me into the force.

"You and your brother are the youngest members of the BEF," she said. "A member of the show you're in will be assigned as your chaperone."

I left wishing I could have learned more about that interesting lady. How did she get into the police force? What kind of work did she do? I'd never met anyone like her. I also wondered how I could prove my new status to the Germans should I be captured. Raf and I never received any kind of identification.

On March 3, we boarded a ferry at Dover on the south coast. It was a beautiful, sunny day. As we left the dock, Raf and I stood on the deck looking down at the water, our eyes glued to what looked like discarded bowler hats but were actually mines bobbing on the surface, just feet from the boat. They'd been placed there by the army in the event Hitler decided to invade England. The atmosphere around us was tense, and no one spoke as the pilot slowly guided the boat through this hazard. I glanced up at the white cliffs of Dover, a sight I never tire of looking at. Some things about the day seemed so normal, but the pilot's careful maneuvering reminded me we were at war. What was ahead for us in France, I wondered. This wasn't going to be my first visit. I had been there many times with my dad when he worked on the French Riviera, in Brittany, Paris and various other cities.

As we approached the French coast, I thought of one particular visit in 1929. My dad was working in Paris, and it was my turn to travel with my parents. They'd also invited my maternal grandmother Sarah to join us. She was recovering from surgery, and my dad wanted to do something nice for her.

One day he left the hotel to do some errands but hadn't been gone more than half an hour when he returned, all excited.

"Get your coats on!" he said. "We're going to see the trenches from the World War I."

We climbed into a taxi and drove for an hour, then stopped in the middle of a big field. The driver pointed, and there were the trenches. As we walked down into them, my dad told me about the terrible carnage that had happened there. I was only seven, but my mind was filled with visions of the graphic photographs of wounded soldiers we had seen displayed all along the Champs Elysee. My imagination went wild as I walked through those muddy trenches, thinking about those poor unfortunate soldiers. Jolted back from my memories, I thought, "Surely that's not going to happen all over again?"

Before we disembarked, we met the other 18 members of the show. George Formby and his wife Beryl were traveling by some other means. There was a Scottish comedian, four girl dancers, a trampoline act and some musicians. My chaperone turned out to be Dorothy, the lady singer. She was very pleasant and took her responsibility seriously, never letting me out of her sight. But oh how I longed to escape from her chain-smoking.

Everyone was thrilled to be in a show with George Formby. He was one of England's top stars, not only of the stage but of movies, radio and the recording industry. He sang songs in his broad Lancashire accent while strumming on his ukulele. One of his most popular songs was "When I'm Cleaning Winders."

Vans met us when we got off the boat at Calais, and we were driven to British Army Headquarters in Arras, close to the Belgian border. We were installed in the same hotel as the officers. There's something to be said for working with a star. We ate in the same dining room as the brass. George and Beryl ate with the generals. We were close enough to hear Beryl's embarrassed, "George!" whenever he slurped his soup. They were such down to earth people, never demanding special treatment. Beryl surprised me one day with a gift of one of her dresses – a glamorous white sequined creation. It was beautiful, and I wore it for years.

Our venues were mostly old, dusty opera houses which had been closed for years. Some enterprising men in our group soon discovered a hidden treasure in each of these theatres – a wine cellar. Viewing it as spoils of war, they forced the doors open and helped themselves to a few samples. I always expected the French Gendarmes to show up and haul away these incorrigible show people, but they never did. The show was a huge success wherever we went. We couldn't help but choke up as we looked out from the stage onto this sea of khaki. Britain had declared war on Germany, but apart from sending troops to France where they established camps behind the massive Maginot Line, it did nothing. American journalists called it "The Phony War." This situation couldn't last forever. Then what? The future for these men was so uncertain. These English "Tommies" were the most appreciative audience anyone could hope to have.

The show opened with "The Four Redheads," girl dancers. They did a fast-paced tap routine. You could hardly hear the tapping for the roar from the men. Neil McKay, the stand-up Scottish comedian, came on next. The boys loved his thick brogue and sly humor. He was followed by Terry Wilson, who before the war was a fixture in summer shows on the piers on English beaches. He was used to working with an audience and led them in a sing-along of old favorites. The girls came on again and danced a beautiful ballet. This had the effect of calming the audience down, which was perfect for Dorothy who followed, accompanied by three male singers. Their harmonies and beautiful voices went over big. Then it was time for our act. Like all the other girls in the show, I received loud, appreciative whistles as I made my entrance. There was no piano, so my dad and I went straight into our patter routine. We couldn't go wrong. Everything we did went over big, and when Raf and my dad did their burlesque tango, I thought the screams of laughter would cause the roof of the theatre to fly off. It created the perfect atmosphere for George Formby to come on and do his act. Just before the curtain went up, Beryl placed six, pre-tuned ukuleles on a table. They were backups in the event of a string breaking or an instrument going out of tune.

When George came on stage, the audience applauded and yelled for two minutes. He grinned in his shy way, and when they quieted down he sang old favorites from his work on stage and in the movies. His soft Lancashire accent and endearing manner plus his accomplishment as a musician was an unbeatable combination.

The show ended with the trampoline act. Dressed as clowns, the two men did amazing tricks and had the audience gasping at their daring. When it was over, George came back on stage and asked if any soldier would like to try his luck on the trampoline. There were always lots of volunteers. The first thing the soldier had to do was take off his heavy army boots. This always evoked a yell from the audience as the poor man invariably had a huge hole in his sock. But it was all in good fun, and after it was over, as a reward for being a good sport, George gave the soldier a pair of hand-knitted socks. We had bags and bags of these socks; all made by ladies back in England who wanted to do "something for our lads." The government supplied yarn to anyone who would knit a pair of socks. I wondered who was wearing the ones I'd made.

During our month in France, the only Germans we saw were in reconnaissance planes that flew over us daily, a reminder that there was a war on, such as it was. Good food was plentiful – a far cry from our rations at home. It was hard to understand why the French had so much more food than we Brits. When we went out to eat in a restaurant, there was a large array of delicious-sounding dishes on the menu. As my father was the only one in the show who spoke fluent French, the cast was forever asking him to translate names of dishes. He got so tired of having his meal interrupted with the constant, "Tommy, what does this mean?" that he would sigh and then tell them, "Just order, une omelette."

Our troops did not share in this bounty. We found that out when we did a show on an army base and ate what they did. On one occasion, I had taken a bite out of a slice of bread. When it came time for the orderly to clear the table, he took my slice of bread, cut off the part where I had eaten, and took the rest back to the kitchen. Nothing was wasted.

The army restricted our movements, so we had no opportunity to sight-see. But, one day, while George went to Paris to perform a charity show with the famous soprano Lily Pons, the army gave us a treat: they drove us to Mont Saint Michel, a little island off the north coast of France, famous as a shrine devoted for 1000 years to Saint Michael. We had to time our visit carefully as the island can be reached only at low tide. We had the place all to ourselves as there were no tourists.

"Be back here in one hour," the driver said.

We were disappointed there wouldn't be enough time to explore the whole island, but it was fun climbing the steep streets and looking into the shop windows. The highlight of the trip for me was a wicked, rich cup of chocolate topped with a dollop of thick whipped cream. All too soon, it was time to get back in the van and drive back to Arras for our show that evening. But when we reported back to the van, the driver took a body count and said, "We're one person short."

I glanced around quickly and said, "It's Neil."

"Wouldn't you know it," someone said. "I bet he's found a pretty mademoiselle."

The driver was concerned. "Will someone go look for him? We really must get going."

Terry volunteered and disappeared quickly up the hill. In about ten minutes, he returned with Neil in tow.

"Where were you?" we all wanted to know.

"Och," he replied, "I met a bonnie lassie. Didnae want to leave."

There was a collective sigh as we climbed into the van. No one was sorry for Neil having to leave his latest conquest. We all knew he'd find another bonnie lassie soon enough.

When our "tour of duty" ended in April, we learned we wouldn't be leaving from Calais as the port was now a fortress and its use by civilians strictly limited. We were driven instead to Cherbourg where a small fishing vessel waited for us. There were no other passengers. This little boat had no cabins and reeked of fish. Luckily, it was a sunny day, and so we sat on piles of oily rope coiled up on the deck and reminisced about our unique experience.

Neil McKay pulled a bottle of cognac from his pocket. He'd saved it for this occasion.

"Here, lassie," he said as he passed me the bottle. "Have a wee sip."

I took a sip and almost gagged. It stung the back of my throat, and I choked as tears ran down my face. Neil laughed and said, "Och! Poor, wee lassie! Pass it on to the others."

I handed the bottle to Dorothy, hoping it wouldn't come around again.

Chugging across the Channel in that little fishing boat was a perfect end to our adventure. It all seemed so peaceful, but as we approached the shore at Weymouth and saw the mines bobbing in the water and the barricades on the beach, we were reminded that these were not peaceful times. Our happy laughter faded away.

Chapter Eight

The first Sunday we were home, we had visitors. Buzz called; said he'd like to come over and introduce his wife to us. I was curious as to what kind of girl he married. It turned out she was pretty and blonde, the opposite of my coloring. By the look on her face, she'd been dragged there. After our introduction, she looked me up and down, then said, "I hear you're on the stage."

"That's right. And what do you do?"

She sniffed and said, "I'm doing work of national importance."

Oh, how insufferable! I knew right then we'd never be friends and was glad they didn't stay long.

The Phony War ended abruptly one month later in May, and the real war started as the Germans began their rampage through Europe. Memories of our time in France came flooding back as we learned of the complete obliteration of our hotel in Arras and the perilous situation of troops we had so recently entertained. France was in utter chaos, and the forced evacuation of our army from Dunkirk occupied everyone's hopes and prayers. Calls on the radio begged for anyone with a boat to go down to the south coast and help with the evacuation. This response by civilians is one of the most heartwarming stories of the war. Dozens of small boat owners responded to the plea and rescued thousands of soldiers under extremely dangerous conditions. No boat was armed, and the Luftwaffe tried hard to sink them.

After Dunkirk, everyone in England was convinced Germany would invade us any day: our army was decimated, its supplies abandoned in France, and our heroic RAF hopelessly outnumbered in pilots and planes. A pall hung over the entire country. I remember going upstairs and looking out the window, wondering what it would be like to see German soldiers marching down the street. How would I act? Would I stay in the house or go outside and glare at them? But as each new day arrived and there were no Germans, we could not believe our luck. Hitler didn't realize he could have just walked right in and taken over.

Hitler's failure to seize the moment finally jolted England into action. Everyone realized what a lucky escape we had had and that it was vital to get better prepared for whatever Hitler had in store for us. The future looked grim, but Churchill with his great oratorical skill rallied the country around him and vowed, "We will never surrender."

The government moved quickly to re-establish army camps. The manufacture of airplanes was dramatically increased, and young men in their teens were recruited for training as pilots. Britons accepted the fact that life would be hard, that war meant sacrifices. But we knew our cause was just and were prepared to fight to the finish.

Although we felt alone in our struggles, we did have a powerful friend on the other side of the Atlantic – President Franklin Delano Roosevelt of the United States. Since 1938, Roosevelt had been aware of the menace Fascism posed to world peace. However, in his own country, he was denounced as a warmonger for his opinions. But despite the general attitude in America against getting involved, hundreds of young American men came to England and volunteered as pilots in the RAF.

When France fell in May 1940, Roosevelt helped the U.K. in every way possible except militarily. The president did his best to keep America out of the war but wanted desperately to help the beleaguered countries defend themselves.

England became the front line as it entered the new phase of the conflict. On June 5, 1940, the British people had a taste of what was ahead for them. The Luftwaffe started to bomb shipping convoys, and the Wehrmacht seized the Channel Islands. The British Government had already decided that defense of those tiny islands would be too costly and had urged the population to evacuate to the mainland. All but 11 of 1,450 people left Alderney, which is just three and a half miles long and one mile wide. To their later regret, many stayed on the larger islands, Guernsey and Jersey. The occupying force made life extremely difficult for the local civilians. The Germans used slave labor to turn the entire island of Alderney into a fortress.

July 10th, 1940, is the recognized date for the start of the Battle of Britain. Bombing attacks increased, and Hitler ordered the German army and navy to prepare for "Sea Lion," the name he gave for his planned invasion of England. On the 19th, Hitler thought he'd be generous and give the U.K. one more chance before he invaded it. His offer was in the form of a conditional peace offering – he would not invade, and Britain could keep its empire if we just left him alone to dominate Europe. He didn't know the British. Lord Halifax, British Foreign Secretary, got on the radio and politely declined his offer.

We braced for what was to come. The government, fearing tremendous human losses, closed all theatres and sports stadiums. This action caused a huge public uproar. Asking the Brits to go to war against Hitler was one thing, but give up their night at the theatre or a football game? Not bloody likely! Life was grim, and the people made it clear they needed something to smile and laugh over. The government quickly caved in and cancelled the order.

However, there was one theatre that never did close. It stayed open throughout the war, never missing a single performance. It was the Windmill Theatre in London, featured in the British film *Mrs. Henderson Pres-*

ents. It was because of the owner Mrs. Henderson's efforts to improve business and her friendship with Lord Cromer, the Lord Chamberlain at the time, that a law was passed allowing nudity on the stage. The law stated that nudity would be allowed so long as no one moved. It had to be a tableau vivant – a living painting. This law affected all British theatres.

Wilf, later my sister Fe's husband, appeared in shows at the Windmill Theatre many times in his equilibrist act. It was exhausting work. There were six shows a day. By the sixth show, everyone was tired out. No one had any energy left.

One night during the last show, Polly, one of the girls, was posed on top of a drum. Unfortunately, being tired, she lost her footing and fell down on to the stage with a big thump. Embarrassed, she burst into tears and ran off stage, not realizing she was breaking the law as she did so.

All the girls at the Windmill were noted for their beauty and gorgeous figures. Comedians, although happy to be surrounded by so many good-looking women, hated working there. The audience had come to look, not laugh. Wilf actually saw some men doing crossword puzzles and reading books when the girls weren't on.

Meanwhile, the war continued. On August 8, 1940, the Luftwaffe launched a three-pronged attack against ports, the radar defense system, and RAF airfields. On every day of that month, at least 1,500 enemy planes crossed the English Channel on their way to destroy some part of England. Despite overwhelming odds and with the help of the newly developed radar detection system barely out of its experimental stage, the RAF shot down two enemy planes for every British one downed. An added advantage was that British planes were more maneuverable than the German's.

Despite this success, overall, England was taking a beating. We lost dozens of our heroic pilots and thousands of civilians. Resentment was building up against the Luftwaffe for all the destruction it was inflicting on us.

"When are we going to retaliate?" people kept asking.

"When are we going to show the Germans what it's like to be bombed every day and every night?"

The government understood this frustration but pleaded a shortage of planes and pilots. We couldn't argue with that, so we stiffened our spines and braced for the next onslaught.

One day at the end of August, the BBC startled us with the news that several squadrons had flown all the way to Berlin and bombed it. This was a huge achievement. It was far more difficult for the RAF to fly hundreds of miles over enemy territory to Berlin than it was for the Luftwaffe to reach its target. Their planes just had to hop over the English Channel from captured French airfields.

Britons cheered at this fantastic news, but Hitler was furious. He'd always told his people they would be safe. The bombing so enraged him that he ordered the Luftwaffe to start targeting London and other cities, and so on September 7, 1940, the Blitz began. It was the first time in modern history that a civilian population was targeted.

The bombing was relentless, and much of London was in flames. I happened to be home one day during a very heavy raid. Suddenly, I heard a roar that sounded like a plane flying low and getting closer and closer. I dashed to the back door and opened it. There, at the bottom of our garden, barely skimming the tops of the trees, was a Messerschmidt! I recognized it from the drawings of different planes in the newspaper every day. The government asked the public to become familiar with configurations of airplanes and to report any lone German plane that might be on a reconnaissance run. I could see swastikas on the wings, and I even saw the pilot. He was looking down from side to side, probably wondering where he could land. I gasped, never thinking I'd ever see the enemy this close. How did he ever get past the barrage balloons, I wondered. His engine sputtered as he lumbered on, weaving his way between the houses. I thought there was no need to report this sighting as it was obvious that this plane would not be airborne much longer.

For a moment, I felt sympathy for this man, so far from home, all alone, about to crash, die or be captured, and doomed to spend who knows how long in a prison camp. Then I reminded myself he was the enemy and had probably killed a lot of Brits. Later, I learned that a German plane had crash-landed on Wimbledon Common, that the pilot, though injured, had survived, and that the Wimbledon Police had captured him.

We had to watch my grandmother during these heavy raids. She had no concept that there was a war going on and loved to stand by a window and admire the colorful flares the Luftwaffe dropped to illuminate its targets.

"So pretty!" she would exclaim. "Oh, mira! Beautiful!"

"Mama! Close the curtains! Get away from the window! Dangerous!"

We had to pull her away. She didn't understand enough English for us to explain what flying glass would do to her if a bomb dropped close by. She couldn't differentiate between the air raid sirens either.

"Comin' or goin'?" she would ask.

Chapter Nine

On a rainy day in August 1940, we reported for duty to ENSA at their Drury Lane Theatre offices. All we were told was that we'd be doing a show at an air base outside London. We never knew the name or the exact location of these bases and didn't want to know. What we didn't know, we couldn't repeat. London was on the frontline of the war, and everyone wanted to act responsibly.

At four in the afternoon, by the back entrance to the theatre, we piled into a van and joined the other performers who would be going with us. There were three girl dancers, a male singer, and a musical trio. Our act would provide the comedy. It was a pleasant surprise to see the Three Redheads again. I looked forward to catching up with their news. The driver poked his head in the van, counted us, and slammed the door shut.

It was a slow drive through the wet and busy streets of London. People were dashing in and out of traffic as they rushed to get home before the nightly air raids began and the blackout law was enforced. No lights of any kind were allowed at night, making travel very difficult. This ban included flashlights, cigarette lighters, trains, cars, bicycles, and any window of a house whose blackout curtains were not closed tightly. We passed the time chatting amongst ourselves, comparing notes about where we'd worked recently.

Within an hour, we were in the country and soon arrived at our destination – a camouflaged facility, surrounded by ack-ack (anti-aircraft) guns. As we pulled up to the guard house, the driver handed our credentials to the guard. He looked us over and waved us into the compound where an RAF corporal was waiting. He gave us a warm welcome and said, "Follow me!" He then led us to an improvised stage inside a small hangar. Some of the audience was already seated.

Our dressing rooms were curtained-off areas to the side of the stage. By six o'clock, all the seats in the hangar were filled. The show wasn't supposed to start until six-thirty, but the men were already stamping their feet and whistling. We'd barely enough time to talk with the musical trio to explain the needs of our individual acts before the show began.

The show opened with the Redheads. Their first number, a tap dance, was a fast routine designed to wake up the audience should it be necessary. In this case, it wasn't. They followed that with solos from each girl, finishing up with "The Lambeth Walk." They received so much applause that it seemed the audience would never let them go. Jack, the singer, went on and had equal success. The men needed little encouragement to join him in such popular songs as "Underneath the Arches" and "Wishing," the latter a great favorite of all the troops. The two acts put the audience in a perfect mood for us.

We started out with the usual patter, then Raf's tap dance, my Carmen Miranda bit, and finally the tango. Raf and I started it, then my dad came on in his usual floozy outfit. Suddenly, a tall American officer in full battle dress, complete with hand grenades hanging from his belt, strode onto the stage and headed for the mike.

"We are under attack!" he barked. "Battle stations, everyone! Civilians to the shelter!"

A thrill of fear ran through my body. At the same time, I felt silly and totally out of place in my bright red dress. I looked over at my dad, dressed in drag, gazing up in awe at this warrior. The weight of his eyelashes made of pipe cleaners caused him to blink, giving him a flirtatious look. It was a sight I'll never forget, and I stifled a hysterical giggle.

The corporal appeared again and led us to a bunker deep underground. It was damp with just a few benches against the wall. We sat in the dark, shivering in our flimsy costumes. All we could hear were dull thumps as bombs reached their targets. Betty, one of the dancers, started to scream, "We're going to be buried in this bunker! I know it!"

"Pull yourself together," said Raf. "Screaming won't help. Just be glad you're down here and not up there."

"He's right," I said. "Come and sit by me. We'll be okay."

I really wasn't so sure about that. I thought about our friends, the McKays, who had been in their government-issued Anderson shelter when it received a direct hit. Betty finally calmed down, and her screams became soft moans. To take her mind off her fear, I turned to Rachel who had married an officer in the Fleet Air Arm and asked after him.

"He's okay," she said, "but he still fears his days are numbered."

I remembered the story she'd told me in France. When John met Rachel, he fell in love with her and asked her to marry him. She told him she liked him very much but didn't love him. He answered that as far as he was concerned, that didn't matter.

"The planes I fly are ancient, with open cockpits. It's just a matter of time before I'm shot down. If you marry me, I will at least have happiness for a short time, and you would be entitled to my pension."

Rachel almost felt like she was doing her national duty by marrying John, but the union proved a success, and she was thankful that so far John had survived. Suddenly, the corporal reappeared.

"The commander has ordered me to get all you civilians off this base," he said. "Let's go!"

Back up the stairs we went. What met us at the top could have been a scene from *Dante's Inferno*. Everything was on fire – buildings, planes and trees. Men were running around in every direction. The base was lit up like opening night at the Palladium in the old days. Bombs screamed down, determined to destroy anything left standing. I was terrified. I grabbed Betty's hand, and we scrambled into the van waiting there for us. The driver took off, breaking all speed records. We tossed from side to side as he careened around burning planes and dodged huge craters. Betty started screaming again, and I wondered if this was the way I was going to die.

All of a sudden, we were on smooth road, tearing along without lights. The deafening roar of the air attack became muted and gradually faded. No one spoke a word on our way back to London. Even Betty was quiet. Stunned by our close brush with death, we were lost in our thoughts – grateful to be alive but worried sick about all the men we had left behind on the base. They couldn't get in a van and leave. We were all very familiar with air raids but had never experienced anything like this. London, too, was being bombed that night, but the main targets were the East End Docks.

We arrived back at Covent Garden in relative quiet and climbed out of the van, exhausted. We discovered to our great relief that someone had tossed in all our belongings. We thought we'd never see our stuff again. I was also glad to know that I wouldn't have to travel all the way to Wimbledon accompanied by my father in drag.

There was a small room at the theatre where we could change clothes. As we were scheduled for an ENSA show the next night, the driver let us leave our costumes and props in the van. We still had our heavy make-up on and would have to take it off at home. We walked to the Underground and bought our tickets. Other passengers didn't quite know what to make of us and gave my dad especially some very strange looks. It wasn't until we sat down and I looked across at him that I saw why.

"Daddy, you're still wearing your eyelashes and earrings!"

With a sigh, he pulled them off and stuck them in his pocket.

The Aquabelles (left to right) Nena, Betty, Lynette, Helen, Tony and Mary

The Water Show — Hula Dance

I don't care if you burn!

At nineteen

Raf Jover

Raf and Tommy

Tuning Up

Photographs 67

I, yi,yi, yi, yi, I like you very much!

Red Riding Hood Pantomime
Garcia Owen — Principal Boy
Nena — Principal Girl

Red Riding Hood
Principal Girl and Boy, Red Riding Hood and Big Bad Wolf

Cast of Red Riding Hood

ENSA cast in France, 1940. George and Beryl Formby seated, Tommy, Raf and Nena just right of center.

Debby, Rogers, the Hendersons and me.

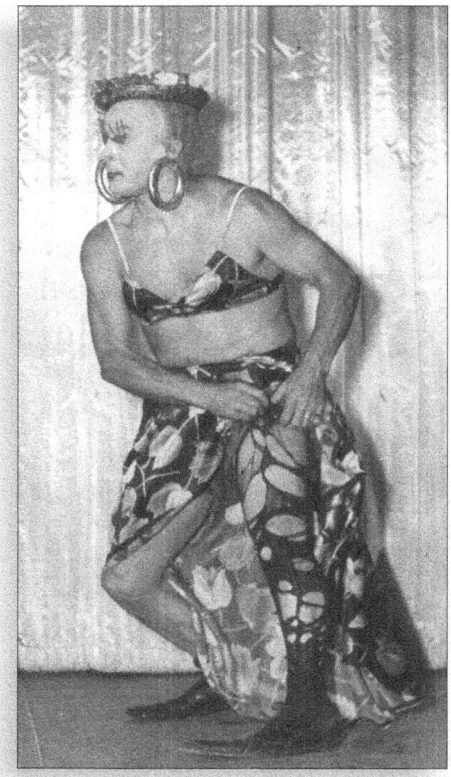

Getting ready for the Tango.

Nena Jover Kelty "Come on, Papa!"

Julian Jover

Raf, front row right, rehearsing with Royal Marine Jazz Band

Julian and Tommy

The family Wolseley and Juanita

Tommy and Julian

Tommy and Teddy Wirnpress

What is this girl doing?

The Spanish Dance

Dick joins the U.S. Navy

Henderson twins, friend, Dickie, Nena

Dick with Pancho

The Tap Dance

"Carmen"

Photographs 81

Working with ENSA

Fe

Fe

... in her red bellboy outfit

Photographs 83

Richard Jover

Mother

Photographs 85

Encounter with Yellowstone Bear

Nena, today

ENSA Performance

My first performance, 7 years old

Chapter Ten

We worked continuously during those nerve-wracking times, traveling to different cities each week, sometimes for ENSA and other times in a regular theatre. Every day, we called home to check on my mother and the children. In November 1940, we were booked to do a week in Dover on the south coast. Only 20 miles from France, you could look across the channel and almost see the enemy without the use of binoculars. November was usually a wet and windy month, but one day it was beautiful – a little chilly, but the sun was out. Not wanting to miss any of those rare comforting rays, I decided to go for a walk. I put my jacket on and picked up a book I'd been reading. I opened the door and started the uphill climb to the cliffs. At the top, there was a bench right on the edge, so I sat down and looked forward to a pleasant hour or two of reading.

After a few minutes, I glanced up and, looking out to sea, noticed a big water spout. What on earth could that be, I wondered. A minute later, there was another one, this time a little closer. Suddenly, I came to my senses, realizing the Germans were shelling! I slammed the book shut and tore down the hill. No wonder I hadn't met anyone on my walk! Most of the German shells had not yet been able to reach the English shore, but I wasn't going to stick around to find out if today would be the exception. I'd also heard that German pilots strafed people as they shopped on High Street. Dover was just as dangerous as London, but in a different way.

Like most people, our family didn't ever talk about the danger we were in or how scared we might be. We knew there was always someone who had it far worse than we did. Survival was a matter of luck, and we were grateful to be alive.

Most of the Dover population had evacuated to safer areas. Many of those who stayed were in the navy. A few had families with them. This was the staging area for rescuing pilots shot down in the English Channel. When a message arrived that a pilot was down, a small, unarmed boat with two men took off to find him. They were told roughly where he might be, but they had to be quick. German pilots would often shoot at the rescuers and even the pilot. It was dangerous and stressful work but vitally important. Saving a pilot was like saving England's first line of defense. Churchill called them "our precious few."

The rescuers comprised most of our audience. They all sported bushy beards and wore bulky warm clothes, looking nothing like the usual immaculate Royal Navy. Many times a message arrived in the middle of a show, and they'd have to dash out. There were very few women.

Occasionally, there was a girl on the bill who did a nude act. When this happened, the other performers always felt a tense atmosphere in the theatre. The audience, though polite and generous with applause, was there for one reason – to see the nude girl. Their impatience was palpable. I was surprised when Shirley, the girl everyone couldn't wait to see, asked if I would do her a favor.

"Would you introduce my poses?" she asked.

She explained that she was an artist's model and was doing the act to make a little extra money. The poses depicted famous paintings.

"I'd appreciate if it you would do this," she said. "There are six poses. I have a script, and you'd just have to read it off stage. I've found that a female voice has a calming effect on the audience. If a man reads it, the audience tends to get raucous."

I was taken aback at first, not sure I wanted to have anything to do with a nude act. However, Shirley didn't look like a girl who would do anything salacious, and I would be hidden from the audience. So I said, "Yes, I could probably do that. May I see the script?"

She handed it to me, pointing out my cues. After glancing at it, I felt better. I couldn't see anything that would embarrass me. I reasoned I could help Shirley out, and the audience would be so busy looking at her that they wouldn't know or care who the narrator was.

I stood on the side of the stage with a mike and watched so that I could come in on cue. Several times I had to ask the stagehands not to block my view. In their determination to see Shirley up close, they would quickly set up the scene for a particular pose, then rush into my small space and jostle each other for a better position. Her act was tasteful and artistic – probably not quite what the audience had anticipated. Shirley's figure was not like those of the slim girls at the Windmill Theatre with their flat stomachs and perky breasts. Hers was perfect for the paintings she portrayed, mostly by the Fleming painter Peter Rubens. She had large breasts and hips and made no effort to hold in her stomach. My task was to describe the painting, tell who painted it, and give a little background. This gave the stagehands time to change the scenery between each pose. For paintings like Ruben's "The Three Graces" and "The Judgment of Paris," the missing characters were painted on the backdrop. The one exception was "The Hermit and the Sleeping Angelica." Shirley, of course, portrayed Angelica, and for the hermit she hired the scruffiest-looking stagehand to stand next to the couch and leer at her. He was the envy of all his fellow workers.

The final pose depicted "Loved Locked Out," a familiar painting to everyone. The backdrop was a picture of an English Victorian garden. There was a gate in one wall, and of course it was locked. Shirley struck a pose, half turned away from the audience and with the back of one hand against her forehead. She was the picture of dejection. The curtain came down to the deafening roar of applause and whistles. Shirley threw on a robe and took several curtain calls. As she came off stage, she thanked me for my help.

"Could you do this for the rest of the week? I really like your voice."

"Of course!"

I was happy to do it, although I thought to myself that "Nude Act Narrator" would never appear on any of my resumes.

After Dover, we went back to work for ENSA. As most of the work was around London, we were able to go home most nights. It was nice getting caught up with our mail and messages.

"By the way," my mother said. "There's one for you from Buzz."

"Buzz? What did he want?"

"He'd like to take you to the pictures."

"What!"

I looked at her in astonishment. "But he's married now!"

"I know. It's all right. He just wants to take you to the pictures. Why don't you go?"

I couldn't believe my ears. My mother, the pillar of virtue, upholder of all righteous behavior, was urging me to go out with a married man. I was totally confused. I'd always thought my mother knew best. Am I the one who is wrong? She finally convinced me that he was just an old friend, and there was no harm in going to the pictures with him. Against my better judgment, I agreed to go.

It was a mistake. In the cinema, he kept putting his arm around me, something he'd never done before. I kept shaking it off, but he didn't give up. It was a disaster. I was angry at my mother and angry at him. I felt manipulated. The film went by in a blur, and we left to go back to my house. It was the longest 30 minutes of my life. When we arrived, I let myself in, slammed the door in his face and stormed up to my room. I threw myself onto the bed, my mind in a turmoil. Was I being too judgmental? Am I a prude? Perhaps Buzz was having problems with his wife. But why would he think I was that available? All these unanswered questions kept me awake, and I hardly slept all night. My mother, who probably heard me slam the door, never asked me how the evening went, and I never saw Buzz again.

Chapter Eleven

With ENSA, we worked under all kinds of conditions. I soon discovered that the armed forces were not prepared for women. On one occasion, we went with a group to an air base near London, where we were met by an officer who led us to an improvised stage. Everyone's luggage, containing their props and costumes, was piled up in the center.

"Please find your suitcases, then follow me," said the officer.

After we'd all claimed our stuff, we noticed a black patent-leather hat box left on its own.

"Whose is that?" I asked. When no one claimed it, a group of us walked over to see if there was any identification. There was nothing.

"Perhaps there's a name inside," someone said. "Take the lid off."

I look the lid off, and we all gasped in unison. "It's a chamber pot!"

The poor officer's face blanched and then turned beet red. "It's for the ladies," he stammered. He led us to our dressing room, which turned out to be a classroom. We draped our costumes over some desks and got ready for the show.

Another time, the stage was set up in a tent – far from any kind of toilet, men's or women's. "We must have a toilet backstage!" the girls insisted.

Two corpsmen scrounged for materials and, with the aid of a couple of sawhorses, a plank of wood, a sheet of corrugated steel and a bucket, came up with a crude but workable device. We applauded their ingenuity and opened the show.

The first act was a troupe of tap-dancers who were lively and noisy, putting everyone in a good mood. They were followed by a man and woman, singing duets. The audience loved the popular songs and, without being asked, joined in. After their act, the orchestra started to play very soft music. The magician, Deveen, looking suave in his top hat, tie and tails, entered stage left, and his assistant, the blonde in "Deveen and Blonde," stage right. Without saying a word, he started to do his sleight-of-hand tricks. Cigarettes appeared mysteriously behind his assistant's ear, a borrowed watch from the audience ended back in the soldier's pocket, and his assistant pulled 20 silk scarves from the magician's sleeve. Then came his disappearing rabbit trick. Still not talking, he indicated to the audience that the rabbit was going to disappear from the table it was on. He used many hand gestures and kept flourishing a black velvet cloth over the rabbit. The audience sat rapt, holding their breath as they watched his every move. Suddenly, the silence was shattered by what sounded like rain on a tin roof. This was followed by laughter coming from backstage and the sounds of panic. An order quickly went out to the cast: "Anyone needing to use the facilities, please wait until the band is playing." A real trouper, the magician kept cool and carried on. The rabbit disappeared from the table and ended up in a cage on another table.

Chapter Twelve

Hitler finally abandoned his plan for invasion and now tried to bomb England into submission. Back in August, the Luftwaffe's first target was shipping, the life line for food and other goods our island needed. Thousands of tons of ships sank before Hitler was convinced he couldn't starve the Brits into giving up. So he targeted airfields and ordered U-boats to focus on shipping. Once again, he was foiled. The heroic RAF, despite being grossly undermanned and with insufficient planes, kept beating back the Luftwaffe.

We worked for ENSA all that summer at army camps and airfields around London. That enabled us to go home nearly every night. One evening, I was helping my mother in the kitchen when we realized that the bombing was not far from us. During air raids, we always had one ear tuned in to the whereabouts of the Luftwaffe. When it was the southwest part of London, we listened extra carefully. Bombs usually came down in sets of threes. After the first one fell, we stopped what we were doing and paid attention to the direction of the second. Was it nearer or farther away than the first? If it was farther away, the plane was not coming in our direction, so we relaxed and went on with what we had been doing. If it was closer, then we could be in trouble. This time, the second one screamed loud as it came down, and we knew we were in the direct path of the third bomb. I reached over, turned off the gas stove, and dove under the table with my mother, sister and little brother. Richard, who was only four, thought this was great fun, four of us hiding under the table. He grinned at my mother, probably wondering who was coming to look for us. Somehow, my mother managed to look calm. We reached for each other's hands.

As we crouched there, I prayed this would not be a direct hit. The air seemed to vibrate as the bomb screamed down. It felt like it was aimed directly at 145 Queens Road. The unbearable suspense ended suddenly with a tremendous bang and the sound of shattering glass. The house shook violently, and the walls seemed to bulge into the room and then back out again. But the house withstood the blast and didn't fall down. And we were still alive! I almost fainted with relief. My mother and I looked at each other. With two little ones sitting between us, we didn't want them to see how afraid we had been.

"Gosh, that was close!" said my mother in as calm a voice as she could manage, as the plane's engines faded away. "Where are Daddy and the boys? I hope they're all right." The words were no sooner out of her mouth when my dad rushed into the room.

"Are you all OK? Raf and Julian were with me in the living room. They're OK. What about Mama and Berry?" Berry suddenly appeared unhurt, and we all went in search of Mama. She was sound asleep in her bed upstairs.

"How on earth could she have slept through all that?" my dad said. "No need to wake her up and tell her what she missed. I'll go over next door and see how the Andrews are. I think the bomb came down in their backyard. Richard, put some shoes on! There's glass all over the place!"

After checking with the neighbors and finding them shaken but safe, Dad came back to assess how much damage we had sustained.

"We're lucky we didn't all get killed," he said. "The bomb came down about 40 feet from our back door."

We walked around the house and took note. Every window had been blown out. I went into my bedroom and gasped. I hadn't yet closed the drapes. One look at my bed, and I realized how lucky I was not to have been in it when the bomb dropped. It was covered with mud and broken glass. I shivered. If I'd been in bed, I thought, all that glass would be sticking in me right now. I suddenly felt weak and wanted to sit down, but there was nowhere to sit that wasn't covered with mud and broken glass. I started to clean up the mess. I couldn't turn the lights on to see what I was doing, but luckily there was a full moon. It took me hours.

In the meantime, the rest of the family was carefully picking shards out of the blackout drapes in the rooms downstairs. None of us got any sleep that night. At about six in the morning, the all clear sounded. There was a big sigh of relief from all of us.

"Well," my dad said, "it could have been worse. Thank goodness we're all safe." Nobody said anything. We realized what a close call we'd had. Although the house had sustained a lot of damage, we'd all survived, and no one was hurt. There was a lot to be grateful for.

"Let's eat some breakfast quickly before they come back," said my mother. I helped her fix oatmeal and toast and our usual coffee. We were lucky there. In a tea-drinking nation, our family preferred coffee which was not rationed. It was contraband – commandeered off enemy ships. We swapped our tea rations for butter or sugar with friends and relatives.

Even though we bundled up in our warmest sweaters, without windows the house was cold. "I'll go down to the Town Hall and see what I can do," said my dad. The local government proved to be very helpful and sympathetic. Someone came out that day to replace the glass.

Later, however, as the Blitzkrieg continued and windows got blown out on a regular basis, things changed. The government replaced only one pane of glass per room. Linoleum was nailed over all the other windows, making the house dark and gloomy. After the first bombing, we noticed that the front wall of our brick house was beginning to pull away, leaving a four-inch gap at the top. The war would have to be over before that would get fixed. We stuffed rags and anything else we could find into the gap to keep the elements out. Other neighbors suffered far worse. Some lost the whole front wall of the house, leaving bedrooms and living rooms exposed. They looked like movie sets complete with furniture and hanging lamps. I always thought about these houses when it was time to have a bath. It seemed as though every time I stripped down and had one foot in the bathtub, the air raid siren would go off. What should I do? Forget about my bath, with its precious five inches of hot water, or risk being part of a movie set in broad daylight, or worse – looking like the center of one of Mrs. Henderson's tableaux?

Everyone handled air raids differently. One of my dad's friends, Senor Monzo, a little Spanish man, took off immediately for the Underground whenever the sirens went off. He didn't even say "Goodbye!" to his wife as he ran out the door. She was left to look after three elderly ladies who lived with them. Another woman in the neighborhood would start screaming. She kept it up until she was exhausted.

"Why doesn't she move out to the country if she can't take it?" my mother said. "She drives me crazy!"

Our family took it in stride. We gave up on the government-issue Anderson shelter my brothers had buried in the backyard. It leaked so badly that we decided to take our chances and sleep in our own beds, preferring to die from a bomb rather than pneumonia. The shelter was too small for our family anyway: it held only four, and there were ten in our household.

Chapter Thirteen

We had no car in those days and had to rely on public transportation to go into and out of central London. The quickest way was to use the Underground which had a station in South Wimbledon, a 15-minute walk from the house. Another option was the train which was closer but did not run late at night. During an air raid, I was terrified of the Underground because the Bakerloo Line, which we used, went under the Thames River. I dreaded being entombed in a watery grave should the station at either side of the river be bombed. Waterloo Station had the scariest entrance. One had to go down two very long escalators to reach the trains. By the time I got there, I could hardly refrain from turning around and bolting up the escalators again.

When the train arrived at South Wimbledon, the doors slid open, and we were greeted with a scene I never got used to. The platform was covered with people sheltered there for the night. Whole families with blankets and pillows put up with the noise and stench of fumes from the trains in order to gain a sense of security. It was something our family never even considered as we lived so far from the station and had so many people in our household. We waded our way through the crowd to the exit, grateful at last for fresh air. I could never live like that, I thought – so claustrophobic. I had to be above ground no matter what.

I thought about those people living their mole-like existence when we went on our next date for ENSA. It was in Aldershot, a huge army base. As it was only about a two-hour train ride from Wimbledon and we would be through working by 8:00 p.m., we decided to commute. After the show one night, we ran for the train and climbed aboard up near the engine which would be closer to the stairs when we exited at Wimbledon. We hummed along for about 40 minutes when the train suddenly screeched to a halt. We poked our heads out of the window but could see nothing. There were no lights on anywhere. We sat there for about 15 minutes until Raf could stand it no longer and had to go see for himself why we weren't moving.

He came running back all out of breath.

"The train's been bombed!" he declared.

"What? How could that be? I didn't hear anything. Did you?"

"No. I think it was the last carriage. They're trying to fix it so that we can get to the next station. They told me to get back on."

We sat there for another half hour until the train gave a little lurch. Several more followed, and then we started to crawl along at about five miles an hour. Finally, we came to a complete stop. We had no idea where we were. All station signs had been removed, of course. The next thing we heard was the engineer walking alongside, shouting, "This is Woking. You can stay in the train overnight or get out and sit in the waiting room. There won't be another train for you until seven o'clock."

We had a quick family discussion.

"Let's get out," said my dad. "Mummy will be worried, and perhaps there's another way we can get home."

I looked at my watch. It was midnight. On his way back to the engine, I asked the engineer if anyone had been hurt by the bomb.

"I'm not sure. I don't think anyone was killed, but they did send for an ambulance."

We soon discovered there was no other way to get home from Woking at that hour. There were no lights on anywhere, and none of us could scrape up the correct coins to make a phone call. We settled down in the waiting room and tried to sleep on its hard wooden seats. Three hours went by when we heard some kind of vehicle pull up outside the station. We rushed outside. There was a man taking stacks of newspapers out of the back of his van and piling them up on the pavement. He was shocked to see anyone up at this hour.

"Our train got bombed, and we can't get home. Are you going anywhere near Wimbledon Station?" asked my dad.

"Yes, as a matter of fact, that's one of my stops."

"Could you give the three of us a ride there?"

"My van doesn't have any seats, just one for the driver. You'll have to sit on newspapers."

"That's OK. We are so grateful."

And with that, we scrambled into the van.

It was a wild ride as the driver was anxious to complete his deliveries before he had to show up for his next job. With nothing to hang on to, we kept sliding off the stacks of newspapers. Finally, we arrived at Wimbledon Station, thanked the driver profusely and started our 10-minute walk down Queens Road. It was 4:00 a.m. My mother was still awake. She had been frantic with worry and almost cried with relief when she saw us.

It was always pitch black as we walked home late at night. There were no lights of any kind; even lighting a cigarette was prohibited. Unless the moon was out or the Germans had dropped flares, we had to feel our way around corners. We couldn't even see each other. Disembodied voices floated through the gloom as people called out to each other, "Where are you?" or "Oops! I'm so sorry!"

We tried to keep track of each other's whereabouts by talking. I called out to my brother, "Hey, Raf! Where are you when I need you?"

"I'm here! What do you mean?"

"Just thinking. D'you remember when you were a little boy, how you guided cars during those pea-souper fogs?"

"Yeah. I walked in front of them with a torch. I think I got tuppence or three pence per car."

"Too bad you can't use a torch now."

"Yeah."

We walked on, each of us lost in our memories, when Raf suddenly shouted, "Ouch! Damn it! I tripped over something squishy."

"Are you hurt?" I said.

"I think my knee's bleeding, but I'm OK."

A few minutes later, we arrived home. Raf limped in and threw a package on the table.

"Is that what you tripped over?" I asked.

"Yes, I can't wait to see what's inside."

We all stood around while he carefully unwrapped layer after layer of grease-proof paper. At last the mystery was unveiled – a glorious, golden pound of butter – one person's ration for two months.

"Black market! Serves them right for losing it!" said my dad. I also had nothing but scorn for anyone who participated in the black market. To my way of thinking, it was traitorous. However, it didn't stop me from enjoying this unexpected bounty, which after sharing it equally meant an extra slice of buttered toast for everyone. Raf felt his sore knee was a small price to pay for the butter. We were always a little hungry, and it was small consolation to hear the government assure us we were healthier because we ate less.

One day, my dad announced, "The London County Council has lifted the ban on owning live stock in London. By forfeiting our egg ration (one a month if we're lucky and the grocer had some), we can get poultry feed for chickens. I think we should do it."

"We don't know anything about raising chickens!" said my mother.

"The last egg I had was stamped 'Czechoslovakia 1939,'" I said. "It sure would be nice to have a fresh egg."

"We can learn how to do it. It can't be hard. Lots of people do it. I'll get a book from the library. With a few scraps from the table, we can stretch the feed and get even more eggs."

There was no stopping my dad when he had an idea. The library book gave him good instructions on how to raise chickens. In two days, with Raf's help, he had completed step #1 – build a chicken coop. Step #2 was buy chicken feed. This was easy after we gave up six of our egg rations. Then came step #3 – buy chickens.

"Which breed are you going to get?" my mother asked.

"What do you mean, which breed? A chicken's a chicken."

"Yes, but some are better layers than others. Doesn't the book tell you what to get?"

"Oh, maybe." He went back to the book and found a chapter on that very subject.

"Rhode Island Red. That's the best layer."

"Sounds like an American chicken. Are you sure you can get that one?"

"I'll find out tomorrow. I'll go to the poultry market, and I'll come home with something."

And he did come home with something – six small Rhode Island Reds. He let them loose in the backyard where they strutted around like they owned the place. Having chickens was such a novelty that we couldn't take our eyes off them. We gave them full range of the yard which was big for a London house. There was a lawn surrounded with oak trees, a mulberry bush at the far end, and various berry bushes. It was fun to watch the chickens after it rained. As they walked around, they picked up so many wet leaves on their feet that it looked like they had plates attached.

Richard eagerly tackled his assignment of searching for eggs every day. Morning after morning he reported, "No eggs."

Suddenly, two weeks later, our early morning peace was shattered with Richard screaming, "I found an egg! I found an egg!"

We gazed in awe at this beautiful creation and wondered who would be the lucky one to eat it. My mother soon removed all hopes any of us might have had.

"I can't do anything with one egg. With no refrigerator, we'll have to preserve the eggs until we have enough for a meal."

We watched as she carefully dipped this little treasure into a solution called water glass, and then placed it in a wire basket. My mouth watered as I gazed at it, trying to recall what a soft-boiled egg tasted like. Our partnership with the chickens was a big success. We fed them. They laid eggs. The day came at last when we had enough eggs to make omelets for everyone. What a feast!

Our routine of feeding, gathering, preserving, and eating, went along smoothly for months until for several days in a row there were no eggs to gather.

"What do you suppose is wrong?" asked my dad.

"Their laying days are over," said my mother. "We'll have to eat them and buy some more chickens."

"Eat them! No! We can't eat them! They haven't done anything wrong!" cried Richard, bursting into tears.

"Come over here, Richard," my mother said. She put her arms around him and tried to console him.

"Richard, dear, we know you love the chickens. We all do, but we can't keep them as pets. That's why people have chickens – so they'll have eggs and food to eat."

"It's not fair!"

"I know. We'll get more chickens, and you can look for eggs again."

"I'm never going to look for eggs ever again," he insisted, as he stomped out of the room.

"Oh, dear, poor little boy," sighed Mummy. "Tommy, the sooner you kill those chickens, the sooner he'll get over it."

"Right. How do I do that?"
"You wring their necks."
"Oh. Well. Uh, that shouldn't be too hard."

Perhaps the chickens knew what was in store for them. They ran around the yard squawking loudly as my dad tried to catch one. Whenever he got close, the hen would fly up in the air, flap her wings and make a terrible racket. Finally, he got a good grip on one. I turned away, not wanting to watch. Minutes went by before I realized all was not going well. My mother was shouting, "Not that way, Tommy!" And my dad answering, "Well, she won't stay still. I can't get a good grip."

I turned around. That poor chicken had got loose but at a price – she was running in one direction, but her head was pointed in another.

"Tommy! Put that poor chicken out of its misery!"
"It's no good, Vi. I can't do it. You'll have to call the butcher."

My mother sighed and ran to phone the butcher. He agreed to come, driving a hard bargain. "I'll kill 'em and pluck 'em if I can have three of 'em when I'm finished."

"That will be just fine," said my mother, who was anxious to get the ordeal over with. I walked away, not wanting to be a witness. The butcher did what he had to do, and the next day we had chicken for dinner. No one spoke as we ate. I tried not to think how endearing the chickens were as they strutted around with the plate-like feet after a rain. It almost seemed poetic justice that the chicken wasn't very tasty. In fact, it was tough.

Chapter Fourteen

1941 was a turning point for our act. Engaging Leslie Grade as our agent proved to be a smart move. He booked us for the next 17 months without a week off. We traveled from Edinburgh, Scotland, to Swansee in South Wales, and all points between. In March, I began to feel very tired, putting it down to our strenuous schedule. After the show one night, I said to my dad, "Daddy, I can't walk to the station."

"What do you mean, you can't walk to the station? It's only a few yards."

"I know, but it was all I could do to get through the act tonight. I don't know what's wrong, I'm just so tired," and with that I slumped to the ground. Alarmed, my dad called a taxi to take us all the way home where my mother fussed over me and put me to bed. The next morning, I dragged myself to the doctor. He took one look at my eyes and said, "Severe liver attack. You have Hepatitis. London is rampant with all kinds of diseases right now. People who've escaped from the Continent are arriving with diseases we haven't seen in years. You could have picked this up anywhere."

I felt rotten, and his words didn't register. I thanked him for the pills and staggered home. There was never any question of my not working. We had been raised not to give in to illness, no matter what it was. There wasn't even a bottle of aspirin in the house. I don't know if the pills had anything to do with it, but after taking one I turned yellow all over. I was now convinced the doctor was right. It was Hepatitis. There was no talk of being quarantined for that disease; only Diphtheria and Scarlet Fever qualified for that then. I broke the news to my dad.

He said, "That's too bad! Do you think you can work? We can take a taxi to and from the theatre every night."

I nodded, too exhausted to say anything. Somehow, by conserving my strength in the daytime and with the luxury of taxis, I was able to work throughout my illness. I only hoped that if the audience did notice the peculiar hue of my skin, they'd blame it on poor lighting.

That episode made more of an impact on my dad than I realized, for soon after he announced, "I think we should buy a car. We can afford one now, and I found out that because of our work the government will allow us enough petrol to drive from town to town. Raf's going to be 18 this year, and when he joins up Julian will take his place. He'll be traveling with us too to learn the ropes."

I looked over at Julian, who didn't say a word. He was a shy boy of 15 and had confided in me, "I know Daddy expects me to take over Raf's part in the act, but I don't want to go into show business."

I was shocked. "But you have to! What are we going to do if you don't? The whole family depends on us!"

He slumped his shoulders and mumbled, "Well, OK. But I don't like anything about show business."

"It's not so bad," I said. "You'll see."

We'd had cars before but were not prepared for what my dad drove up in one day. It was a black, shiny, pristine Woseley limousine which looked about 50 feet long.

"Where did you find that?" I gasped.

"A rich lady had put it up on blocks for the duration. She can't buy petrol, and her chauffeur is in the army, so she decided to sell it." We all climbed inside, exclaiming over the luxuries.

"Leather seats! There's a pane of glass between the driver and the passengers in back! And a speaking tube! We can give orders to the driver!"

"Well, I'm the driver, and you won't be giving me any orders!" said my dad.

We knew that, but heaven help anyone else who sat in that seat. We continued with our exploration.

"Look at the fold-down seats in the back! And silver vases for flowers!"

We couldn't get over all that luxury or the fact that we owned such a vehicle. My dad said, "We can bring Pancho with us now. Then Mummy won't have to look after him while we're away."

Pancho was our English Bulldog. I was not excited over the prospect of sharing our newly-acquired limo with Pancho. Some of his habits were not exactly socially acceptable. But my dad loved him, and in his eyes Pancho could do no wrong.

There was no garage, of course, at our 19th-century house, but there was someone around the corner who had a large shed he was willing to rent. Life was going to be a lot easier with our limousine. It meant the end of long walks from the train station late at night and endless hours in cold waiting rooms.

Things changed dramatically on the warfront also. On March 11, 1941, President Roosevelt, with his tenacity and powers of persuasion, convinced the U.S. Congress to pass the Lend/Lease Act with an appropriate $50 billion. This was to benefit 38 countries; England received over $31 billion. America geared up its manufacturing of military goods and even its production of food.

These generous acts were greatly appreciated by everyone in England. It not only meant that we'd have the necessary tools to conduct and win the war, but civilians on the home front would have a little variety in their diet. Things like dried milk and eggs, spam and tins of ground pork started to appear on grocery shelves. My mother made a delicious pie with the ground pork, using the fat surrounding it to make the crust. If anyone knew about cholesterol, they didn't mention it.

Even our work was more pleasant. Leslie Grade created a small traveling revue with his own acts, and so for months on end we worked with the same people. It was a rare opportunity for us to get to know our co-workers. Our favorites and the ones with whom we worked the most were the Hendersons – a talented family who did three acts. Dick, the father, did a stand-up routine; which he ended by singing a beautiful rendition of "Tiptoe Through the Tulips." His pretty identical twin daughters, Tricia and Winnie, sang harmony, and his son, Dickie, also sang. Dickie Henderson would go on to become a famous comedic TV and movie star in England.

As we kids were all close in age, we hung around together in the daytime, playing tennis or swimming. Dickie and I, who were the same age, liked each other immediately. We never really went on dates, as we always went out in a group with our brothers and sisters, and of course we'd see each other at the theatre every night. His sisters often spoke of our getting married some day, but neither of us was anywhere near ready for such a big step. The show ended in November, and we all went our separate ways.

On December 7, 1941, Japan made its infamous attack on Pearl Harbor. Hitler was euphoric. All he could think of was that he had a new ally, one that had not been defeated in 1500 years. He gave no thought to the effect that action would have on the people of America. It galvanized the country. The American Congress realized that Japan had joined the Fascists, and therefore America had no choice. Fascism had to be defeated. The next day, America declared war on Germany. This was followed on December 11 by Germany declaring war on the United States of America. Roosevelt asked Congress to declare a state of war.

Chapter Fifteen

The first few months of 1942 went by in a blur. Having the car was sheer bliss. We felt spoiled traveling in such luxury. However, Pancho brought us down to earth regularly with his odorous contributions.

We were working at Golders Green Empire Theatre in London when Leslie Grade paid us a visit. He had some good news. "I've booked you for four months this summer in a show at the Winter Gardens Theatre, Blackpool. It's a George Black production."

My dad was very pleased. He said to us, "Do you realize that George Black is the foremost producer in England? That says something about our act. Somebody likes it."

"Four months in one place!" I said. "We can live like normal people."

"I'll bring the whole family up here and rent a house," my dad said.

With such a wonderful event to look forward to, the next few weeks dragged by, but May finally arrived. We drove up to Blackpool, a seaside resort on the northwest coast of England. The Winter Gardens was a huge entertainment complex consisting of a theatre, a circus, a dance ballroom and various restaurants. It was a favorite vacation destination for coal miners who lived around Manchester and Liverpool.

We had a week of rehearsals before opening night. Raf and I had never been exposed to all the preparations necessary for a big show, and we were fascinated. We learned how important costumes, music, lighting, scenery and timing were to a successful production. George Black attended every rehearsal. He was a tall, distinguished-looking man with steel gray hair and intense dark eyes. Nothing escaped him, and his attention to detail was impressive.

Apart from our participation in the opening and finale, all Dad, Raf and I had to do during these rehearsals was walk through the act for the purpose of music and lighting. Dress rehearsal on Friday went smoothly with only a few glitches. Opening night followed, and everyone was nervous, hoping that nothing would go wrong that might affect their individual part. The curtain rose on *Black Vanities*, with a fast-moving scene introducing the whole cast. When it was over, I went up to my dressing room. As I doubled-checked my costumes, making sure there were no rips needing attention, I listened to the inter-com. Apart from the usual 15- and 10-minute warnings to various performers, I could also hear how the audience was reacting. It sounded like everything was going well; there was lots of applause.

We closed the first half, and as we had costume changes and props to be concerned about, we went down early. Stage hands had erected a temporary place off stage for my quick changes. The piano and props were in place, and we were ready. The curtain went up, and I immediately felt the audience was having a good time. Every part of our act – the comic patter, Raf's tap dance, my Carmen Miranda bit and piano solo – went well, and Dad's burlesque tango with Raf brought screams of laughter from the audience. We had to go back for two extra curtain calls. We felt we had done our part toward making the show a success.

When the show was over, George Black came backstage with a big smile on his face. After congratulating everyone on a job well done, he looked over at us and said, "Tommy! I'd like to see you in my office!"

Raf and I looked at each other. What could be wrong? After about 10 minutes, dad emerged from the office looking dazed. "You're not going to believe this," he said.

"What? What?"

"We're opening at the London Hippodrome on Monday!"

"What do you mean? I don't understand! We're here for four months! What did he say?"

"Sit down and I'll tell you. George Black saw the act for the first time tonight. He likes it very much and asked me, 'How would you like to work at the London Hippodrome?' So I said, 'We'd love to of course.' Then I said, 'When would we do that – after this show's over?'– and he said, 'No, next week on Monday. I really need a strong act in that show. You'd be perfect.' So I asked him, 'Well, what about this show? We're supposed to be here for four months.' And he said, 'Oh, you can come back next year and do it.'"

The three of us were in a state of shock. Things were happening so fast. We were thrilled at the prospect of going into *Get a Load of This*, one of London's top shows. This was big time.

There were a million things to do. First, we said goodbye to all the people in the show. They were as stunned as we were but congratulated us and wished us luck. Then we had to pack everything up and tell our landlady we'd be leaving in the morning instead of four months later. She was disappointed but cheered up after we compensated her. We could grab only a few hours sleep before we had to drive back to London.

"It's good we didn't bring the family up sooner, or we'd have even more stuff to pack," said my dad. "I phoned Mummy, and she's thrilled about the whole thing."

Chapter Sixteen

We arrived at the Hippodrome Theatre on Monday morning as George Black had instructed. No one was expecting us or had even heard of us. In fact, the doorman laughed and said, "Someone's playing a joke on you."

Trying not to get annoyed, my dad told him to call George Black's office. Finally, the doorman was convinced, and he let us in. Things happened fast after that. The music director arrived, then the electrician and even George Black himself. He explained we'd have to make a few changes in the act because of the type of show it was.

"There's no curtain. The stage is a permanent nightclub scene. Nena, we'll have to cut out your piano solo. But I have something else in mind for you. We'll talk to you about it later."

What in the world would that be, I wondered. We were shown our dressing rooms where we hung up our costumes and laid out our make-up. Then we drove home to rest up for a couple of hours before the show. Our spot was in the second half, so we didn't have to arrive early. No one in the show knew we were coming, but they all gave us a warm welcome. One girl pulled me aside and whispered, "Watch out for Vic Oliver!" He was the star of the show.

I said, "What's the problem?"

"He's after every girl in the show. He's worked his way through the whole chorus."

"Thanks for warning me."

Vic Oliver, a titled Austrian, arrived in England via America. He was a skilled violinist, but in his music hall appearances he played badly while telling raucous jokes in his strong accent. In addition, he was famous for his quotations, one of which was about money. "If a man is after money, he's money mad. If he keeps it, he's a capitalist. If he spends it, he's a playboy. If he doesn't get it, he's a ne'er to well. If he doesn't try to get it, he lacks ambition. If he gets it without working for it, he's a parasite. And if he accumulates it after a lifetime of hard work, people call him a fool who never got anything out of life."

Vic was married to Winston Churchill's daughter, Sarah. He was not faithful to her. A parade of young girls came through the stage door every night identifying themselves as "Mr. Oliver's secretary." They didn't fool anyone.

In between shows one evening, the music director came by and wanted to talk to me. I knew and dreaded what was coming. I'd already heard the gossip about the blind pianist suing the theatre. During intermission, he played on a piano that rose up out of the stage. One evening, after he had finished, he was lowered too quickly, causing him to fall and hurt himself. He was replaced with a pit musician who did not relate to the audience at all, keeping his eyes glued to the keyboard. The management was not happy with him.

"Mr. Black wants me to hear you play. If I give the OK, he'd like you to play during intermission. He'll pay you ten pounds a week."

I groaned to myself. I did not want this job. The money would be nice, but although I loved music I did not want to be a professional musician. But how could I say, "No, thank you" to George Black for offering me a job any other pianist would long to have and who had just put us into this fabulous show? So I went along and did my audition. And when the director said, "OK," I said "OK" too.

The next morning, I sat down at the piano and worked up a 10-minute routine of my best pieces. These were jazz transcriptions of old favorites written by very talented pianists. I had no trouble playing what other people wrote but could not improvise. It didn't come naturally to me. However, I practiced like mad and hoped that my memory would never fail me. The next night, I was on, so I showed up underneath the stage and met Joe who would press the button that would raise me up. On cue, I appeared through the stage in my white-sequined Beryl Formby gown, seated at a white piano. The spotlight hit me, and I was on my own.

This was a lot different from my left-hand solo. I was playing for a sophisticated London audience in a genre I was not comfortable with. I hoped I wouldn't embarrass myself.

The house lights were on, so I could see everyone's face. It was unnerving. I could also see Vic Oliver roaming around talking to people in the audience. I was chagrined to see how close the front row was – less than six feet away. Being wartime, this was usually filled with young military officers from different countries. They were probably equally amazed to find themselves so close to a 19-year-old show girl. As I smiled and played my set routine, I said a silent prayer, "Please don't talk to me or request anything." If they did, I knew I'd be lost. I had to concentrate. Most of the time, my prayers were answered, but one night there was a disturbance created by a Danish Naval Officer who would not leave my side. As his friends tried to pull him away, he kept saying, "I need her for my girlfriend!" Finally, his friends were successful, and they all left for the bar. I was a wreck.

Vic Oliver told me later that the most frequent questions he got from the audience as he walked around were, "Can you fix me up with a date with her? (No.) And, "Are her earrings real diamonds?" (No, they were crystal: my mother found them in an antique shop.) I was grateful to

Vic for protecting me. As far as I was concerned, he was always a gentleman. Having my father and brother in the same show didn't hurt either.

Long after we left this show, Raf told me who the blind pianist was that I had replaced. It was none other than George Shearing, jazz pianist, composer and bandleader of legend. Even though at that time he was only 22 and not yet famous, I was grateful to have been ignorant of his identity.

We had barely started at the Hippodrome when my dad received a message from the head office. "Would Nena please use a different song for her Carmen Miranda impersonation?"

I was stunned. "Whatever for? What's wrong with 'I, yi, yi.....'?"

My dad said, "Well, as you know, Tommy Trinder is starring in George Black's other show at the Palladium, and he also does an impersonation of Carmen using 'I, yi, yi.....'"

"But he's a comedian! Mine's nothing like his! And he's even in a different theatre!"

"Mr. Black isn't telling you to cut it out. He just wants you to change the song."

"What could I use? I haven't heard her sing anything else in English."

My dad, who'd met Carmen when he worked in Rio de Janeiro said, "Well, we have one of her records at home. It's called 'Tico-Tico.' She sings it in Portuguese. You could do that."

I knew better than to argue with him. He would never consider the mere fact I didn't speak Portuguese as any kind of handicap. The next day, he played the record for me. There was no way I could sort out all those strange sounds, let alone reproduce them.

"You'll have to find someone who speaks Portuguese to help you," said my dad. "That's one language I don't speak."

It was up to me to find someone. I didn't know where to start and out of desperation called the Portuguese Embassy. The secretary who answered was sympathetic and offered to send someone to the theatre the next day to help me. I was overjoyed. Perhaps this would work out after all. Ten o'clock the next morning I was at the stage door with my "Tico-Tico" record and a wind-up gramophone. A good-looking, 30-something man with piercing dark eyes was already there. We introduced ourselves and went inside. I led Carlos to the stage where under a single light bulb two chairs and a table were already set up for us. He listened to the record and wrote down the words. Then he slowly read them to me as I wrote down what I heard phonetically. Line by line, I read it back to him, and he corrected my pronunciation. After about an hour, he said, "You sound good. Just keep practicing." I was relieved and so grateful.

"Thank you so much! I wish there was some way I could thank you!"

He looked startled, and an eager look came over his face. Not saying a word, he took two steps toward me and looked straight into my eyes. There was no mistaking what he had in mind.

"Oh!" I said to myself. I shouldn't have gushed like that. "Thank you so much! I'll walk you to the door!" I trilled and almost ran to the exit. I said, "Thank you and goodbye" in as calm a voice as possible. He looked at me, nodded and disappeared into the crowd on the sidewalk.

Changing the song didn't seem to make much difference to the audience reaction. But I was more comfortable singing in English, and perhaps the audience would have liked to have understood the words. It was not long before my Carmen Miranda bit came under attack again. And again because of Tommy Trinder. Bebe Daniels, the American movie star who had a featured spot singing in *Happy and Glorious* at the Palladium, was seriously ill.

"Would you fill in for her for three weeks?" Black asked my dad.

"You mean in addition to the Hippodrome?"

"Yes. Do you think you can do it?"

"I think so. It'll be hard, but we can do it."

"Oh, and another thing," Black said. "Nena won't be able to do Carmen Miranda because of Tommy Trinder's bit. Tell her to work up another number, and I'll have a new costume made for her – whatever she wants. I'll pay for the music too."

I was sorry to hear Bebe Daniels was ill. She had enjoyed a long career in silent movies and made a successful transition to talkies. She worked with Harold Lloyd, Cecil B. DeMille, Rudolph Valentino and others. She was married to Ben Lyon, another movie star (*Wages of Virtue, For the Love of Mike, Hell's Angels,* etc.). After their movie careers faded, they formed a Vaudeville/Variety act and took it to England where they were an instant success, appearing on stage and radio. The British people loved them not only for their talents but because they stayed in England throughout the war, putting up with the bombing and lack of luxuries just like everyone else.

I had no idea what to do in place of Carmen. Once again, I felt I was being pushed beyond my capabilities. But, as usual, my dad was confident and had an idea. "I think we should look for a number you can sing using a French accent. You could be like a little coquette. I know George Black will come up with a cute costume for you. You'll do fine. Don't worry. I'll help you." I didn't know if I could act like a French coquette, but so far my dad's ideas had all worked out. He was always telling me, "You can do it! You can do it!"

We went to several music shops and browsed through stacks of sheet music until we found something we thought would work out. It was called "Come on, Papa." Then I went over to George Black's wardrobe department and talked with the head seamstress. She knew exactly what I needed and drew a rough sketch.

"That's perfect!" I said. At least I was going to look good. The costume would be made of red taffeta – very short, form fitting, with frilly white panties showing. Topping it off was a cute little hat.

I went home feeling better about the whole thing. My dad helped me with the French accent. He wasn't a bit worried, but I wished my debut didn't have to be at the London Palladium. Why couldn't it have been at a smaller theatre where, if I messed up, it wouldn't matter so much?

There was nothing I could do, so I put my worries aside and checked all my costumes to make sure they were in good repair.

Those three weeks were hectic. After the first show at the Hippodrome, we hopped into a waiting taxi and dashed off to the Palladium, did a show there, then returned to the Hippodrome to repeat the process all over again. There were compensations – at the Palladium I had Bebe Daniel's dressing room just off stage and her personal dresser, Amy, for whom I was so grateful. My new costume had hooks all the way down my back. My mother, a former dancer, understood everything about quick changes and had designed my Miranda outfit so that I could get in and out of it quickly without help. It was too bad there was no time to enjoy the over-stuffed chairs and private bathroom.

The first time I did my new number, I was so nervous my legs were shaking, so I was surprised and gratified to hear applause at the end of it. After I'd calmed down, I had to admit it was fun doing something new. Several other acts filled in for three weeks at a time for Bebe until she was well enough to return to *Happy and Glorious*.

Chapter Seventeen

I thought that a long stay in the same city would help improve my social life. It didn't. I worked while most young people were out on dates. Even if I removed my make-up quickly, I couldn't get out of the theatre much before ten o'clock. The last train for Wimbledon left at eleven. The Underground ran much later, but taking that meant walking home half a mile, alone, in the dark, in the small hours of the morning. That, plus the likelihood of an air raid made dating in London almost impossible for me.

I thought this was about to change when Celia Lipton, the singer in the show, invited me to a party. It was to be held on a houseboat moored in Maidenhead, about 40 miles west of London on the River Thames. We would be picked up by limousine.

She said, "This man I met is very rich. He's a Captain in the Royal Navy and wants to throw a big bash before he re-joins his ship."

At first I was thrilled. It sounded exciting and a lot of fun, but I had some questions: What time will it be over? Where would I sleep if it goes on until the early hours? How would I get home afterwards?

Celia really didn't have answers, and I began to feel uncomfortable. I gave it some thought and finally declined the invitation, wondering what I was missing and if I was being overly cautious.

I had my answer the next day as I opened the *Evening News* on the train on my way to work. Across the front page, huge bold letters read, "Man Impersonating Officer Arrested at Lavish Party." The article went on to say that in response to complaints of excessive noise, the police in Maidenhead investigated and consequently arrested Rex Barkley, the host of the party causing the disturbance. They determined he was a fraud. Not only was he not a member of the armed forces, but he owed several thousand pounds for renting the boat and several limousines. He'd also run up a huge bill for wine, liquor and various refreshments. The police stated that 20 guests, including several celebrities, were taken to the police station for questioning. Then it listed all their names, and there was Celia's.

When I saw her at the theatre, I told her I'd heard the news. She was so embarrassed. "You were smart not to go," she said. "It was awful! We were all taken to the police station where they asked us what we knew about this man. I told them everything he had told me, which was just a big pack of lies. What a crook!"

Celia was a nice girl, and I knew how upset the episode must have made her. She was a tall, willowy blonde with a lovely singing voice. Her records and CDs are still available today. Her father, Sidney Lipton, was a well-respected musician who apart from five years in the armed services led his dance orchestra for four decades at the Grosvenor House Hotel in London. Today, Dame Celia Lipton-Farris lives in Florida and was honored recently by Queen Elizabeth for her philanthropic work.

Get a Load of This stayed at the Hippodrome for another six months before it was replaced with another show. It was still popular, however, so George Black moved it to The Prince of Wales Theatre for another three months. Time was needed to remodel the stage to accommodate the show, so we went up to Leeds in Yorkshire to work for a week before rejoining the cast.

With an eye to the future, my dad thought this would be a great opportunity to try Julian out in Raf's role. There was a year to go before Raf would be called up, but he was anxious to join the Royal Marines. Julian had been rehearsing for months to take his place.

At band call Monday morning, the theatre manager told my dad that Miss Cissie Williams, booking head for Moss Empire Theatres, phoned asking for a report on the "new Raf." Dad told him that Julian would do the performances on Saturday when he could make his assessment. In actuality, the opposite occurred; Julian worked all week, but Saturday night Raf took over.

All of us could hardly keep a straight face when the manager came backstage to congratulate Raf on his debut stating he was even better than the original. Their having the same build, height and coloring confused a lot of people. It was to be a smooth transition.

Chapter Eighteen

When *Get a Load of This* finally closed, we went back to our usual touring around the country. Our agent, Leslie Grade, booked several acts together, so we again found ourselves working with the same people week after week. I became very friendly with Yolanda Truzzi who with her brother, George, did a juggling act.

Their father had owned the Truzzi Circus, the most famous in Russia. Wherever they went in their country, they were treated like movie stars. When their father died suddenly, his wife decided to leave Russia with her two young children. The thought of running this huge circus all by herself was overwhelming. She wanted to go to another country where the name Truzzi wouldn't bring such unbearable pressure on her. However, leaving Russia would not be easy. Hardly anyone was given permission to do so. She persuaded the authorities to allow her to leave just long enough to try out a new act before putting it in the Truzzi Circus. They gave her permission, which was highly unusual for the times. What she didn't tell them was that she would not be returning. She sold all her assets, invested the proceeds in diamonds and sewed them into the hems of her dresses. The little family crossed the border without incident and made their way to England, where they began a new life. To support the three of them while the children went to school, Mrs. Truzzi formed a dog act and worked in a circus.

Yolanda, with whom I shared a dressing room, was one of the most beautiful girls I have ever met. She was tall and had a regal air about her. She encased her thick blonde hair in a black velvet-crocheted snood, a fashion of the time. When she turned her big, blue, soulful eyes rimmed with long black lashes on to a man, he was rendered speechless. I always thought she should be wearing a crown and ruling an exotic kingdom somewhere. But she was down to earth with the same frustrations and problems just like everyone else.

One day, Yolanda and George were invited to the Russian Embassy in London for dinner. Someone there had recognized the name. She told me that she panicked when she sat down at the table and saw the huge array of silverware. The first dish was served, and she had no idea which implement to use. As she was the only female there, everyone waited for her to start. A kind gentleman, sensing her dilemma, quietly reached for a fork. She quickly followed suit. As much as she enjoyed the evening and the good food, it was a relief when it all ended and she could return to her own element – the theatre.

We used to commiserate with each other over our lack of boyfriends. I said to her one day, "I know that we're on the move all the time, and it's difficult to meet anyone, but I think it's more than that. I think I'm too picky. I haven't met anyone yet I wanted to spend a lot of time with. How about you, Yolanda?"

She sighed, and in her rich Russian accent said, "Ah, yes, Nena. I teenk my heart is made from stone."

"Oh, Yolanda, some day you're going to meet someone. He'll be very rich, and you'll live happily ever after."

"I hope so."

Many years later, on a visit back to the U.K., I remembered that conversation as I tried to come to terms with the news that Yolanda had married a lion tamer. My dream of her ruling an exotic kingdom was shattered.

Chapter Nineteen

We continued touring until it was time to fulfill our contract in Blackpool in June 1943. This time, we were sure we'd be there for the whole season. My mother rented a very nice house, and the family looked forward to being together in a city that was free from bombing and where we could lead a more or less normal life. Raf was now in the Royal Marines, and Julian was doing just fine in his place. It was a lot of pressure for such a reluctant 16-year-old to be under, but he was professional in his attitude and adjusted quickly to his new life.

During the week of rehearsals, we got fitted for costumes for the opening scene and were assigned dressing rooms. I was sharing with two girl dancers. The room was small and crowded with all our stuff. There would be lots of time between the opening of the show and our act, so I knew I'd have to find something to do to keep out of the girls' way as they made their numerous changes.

We're All In It had its opening night and, judging by its reception, would enjoy a successful season. I started to explore the Winter Gardens complex and found a little coffee shop right next door to the theatre. Perfect. This would be my little haven away from the crowded dressing room. I got into the habit of going there with a book during every show. I sat at a corner table and usually had the place to myself.

One evening, I noticed an American Army officer sitting at another table. After a few minutes, he came over and asked if he could join me. I nodded, and he introduced himself. He was Colonel Charlie Himes, a pilot from Selma, Alabama. He was such a gentleman, and I loved that southern drawl. With my full stage make-up, he could see I was in the show, and it wasn't long before he asked if I would do him a favor.

"Yes, if I can."

"Well," he said. "Last week, I met this wonderful girl. She's in the show, too. Her name is Margo. Do you know her?"

"Yes, of course. She's one of the dancers."

"If I wrote a little note, would you give it to her?"

"Yes, I'd be happy to."

He pulled out a notebook and proceeded to write. I waited, hoping this nice man wasn't too smitten with Margo. I couldn't tell him that she was having an affair with the comedian in the show. He folded the note and thanked me profusely.

"Don't mention it," I said. "If Margo answers, I'll bring her note with me next time. I come here every evening about this time."

He thanked me again, and we shook hands. For the next few weeks, I acted as Cupid, carrying notes back and forth between Charlie and Margo.

On one of those occasions, Charlie brought a friend with him, Lieutenant Shaddock. While drinking coffee together, they told me their base in Freckleton was having a dance that Saturday night and asked if I'd like to go. Shaddock would pick me up.

"Yes, I would," I said. This is already a big improvement on London, I thought.

Charlie and Shaddock arrived Saturday night with disappointing news.

"The dance has been cancelled. We couldn't find enough girls to come. Would you like to come back to the base instead and have a rum coke?"

I was disappointed about the dance but had heard about rum cokes and was curious.

"Yes, I'd like that."

"Where's Margo?" Charlie asked.

"She's not coming – something about a previous engagement."

He looked crushed. He's better off without her, I thought. When I asked Margo why she wasn't coming, she said, "He's so boring! It takes him forever to say something."

"Well, I think he's a very nice man," I said, and left it at that.

We got in the Jeep and drove for about 20 minutes to Wharton Air Base. We entered the Officers' Club, and I noticed right away a man dressed in civilian clothes amongst all the pilots. As I chatted with Shaddock, my eyes kept drifting over to him. Who is he, and what is he doing here? I wondered. I couldn't get over how relaxed and at ease he was with everyone. He didn't sit in the chair so much as drape himself over it. What an attractive man. I glanced at his left hand. No ring. I wondered if he had a girlfriend. I also noticed that he was missing the tops of two fingers on that hand. How did that happen? I took in everything about him – his wavy black hair, soft brown eyes and the friendliest grin I'd seen on anyone.

Suddenly realizing I must be staring, I turned back to Shaddock and took a sip of my rum coke. Just then, Charlie walked by. He said, "Nena, I have a friend I'd like you to meet. Stay there. I'll bring him over."

It was the civilian! Up close, he was even more attractive. He had a handsome, open face, and when he grinned at me my heart started to pound.

"Dick Kelty," he said as he stuck out his hand. "Charlie's told me so much about you. We're coming to the show tomorrow night. I'm looking forward to seeing it. We have front row seats."

I gulped. Most performers don't feel comfortable having someone they know in the audience, and I was no exception. I wondered what he'd think of what I do. Would he think it was frivolous? Why is it so important what he thinks? I asked myself. We shook hands, and he went back to his chair. I had another rum coke and tried to pay more attention to Shaddock who, after all, was my date. After a couple of hours, the party was over, so he drove me home. I thanked him and hoped that as far as he was concerned the evening hadn't been a total disaster.

The next night, after the show started, I peeked through the curtain. There were Charlie and Dick in the front row. But what happened? Dick was wearing dark glasses and had his arm in a sling. I couldn't wait to find out the next day when I'd see Charlie in the coffee shop to get my answer. I got through the act somehow, trying not to make eye contact with those two grinning Yanks in the front row. I'd never felt so self-conscious.

"It was my fault," Charlie said. "We were flying back from Ireland, and I was at the controls. I misjudged the end of the runway, and we crashed. Dick got banged up a little. He has two black eyes and a sprained arm."

"Oh, gosh!"

He leaned over the table and, looking straight into my eyes, said, "Ya know, Dick really likes you. He wants to see you again, have a date. Would you come back to the base again tonight? There's really nowhere else to go at that time. I could drive you there, and he'll drive you home. How about it?"

"Why, Charlie! You're playing Cupid now! Yes, I'd like to see Dick again. Does he have a girlfriend?"

"Nope. He dates, of course, but there's nobody special."

"All right. I'll see you later. I have to go now. Do you have a note for Margo?"

"No. She didn't answer my last one. I don't know what's going on."

"I'm sorry, Charlie. See you later."

I went back to my dressing room and started to touch up my make-up. As I added more mascara, I thought, Why couldn't I have met Dick four months ago? We only have one more week in Blackpool. Next week we're off on our usual touring – a different city every week. Just my luck!

When we arrived at the Officers' Club, Dick met us and led us to a table. Charlie excused himself, said he had letters to write. After we sat down, I asked Dick what he was doing at Wharton Air Base. He told me he was only there for a couple more days, and that he worked for Lockheed as a liaison with the Air Corps.

"Where are you based?"

"In Ireland. I have a contract for two years."

"What happens after that?"

He grinned and said, "That depends on a whole lotta things. I'll have to wait and see what my options are."

I was really curious to know more personal things about him, but my English upbringing frowned on asking such direct questions. I was glad when he began to tell me about himself.

I learned he was 24, that he lived in California, had a widowed mother and two brothers, and that he loved the outdoors. He saw me glancing at his hand with the two missing fingers. "Oh, that," he said. "I did that when I was 19. I was making a bomb in the garage with my friends for the Fourth of July."

"Why on earth were you making a bomb?"

"It was a dumb thing to do. I should have known better. And being the instigator of the fiasco, I was the one with his head over it as I tamped down the explosive. I not only lost two fingers but the sight in my right eye as well. It was really hard on my mom as my dad had died just three months before. I'm the only son still at home. Both my older brothers are married."

As he talked, I found myself getting more and more attracted to him, but my mind kept telling me, Look, this is only a date. You'll be gone next week. Don't get your hopes up.

He interrupted my reverie with, "OK. Now it's your turn. Tell me all about yourself."

I told him about my parents, my two sisters, three brothers, and the crazy business we were in. I explained how we were on the move all the time.

"Next week, I'll be 21, and we'll be working in Brighton on the south coast. After that, we have to fulfill our obligation to ENSA for a few weeks. We don't know where that will be. Will you write to me?" I asked, feeling very forward.

He laughed, "Of course. What did you think?"

"Well, I didn't know if…."

"Don't worry. I'll write. Just tell me how I can reach you."

I gave him my home address and that of the Hippodrome in Brighton, and he gave me his.

It was almost curfew time, and I had to get off the base, so we borrowed Charlie's jeep, and Dick drove me home. He parked in the street and walked me up to the door. We stood there holding hands, looking at each other. I think we both realized that this was more than a casual encounter. He pulled me forward and wrapped his arms around me. Neither of us said a word. Then he kissed me. I thought my legs would give out. My whole body down to my toes felt a thrill. I thought, my life will never be the same. I never thought I'd meet anyone like him. I don't know how this will ever work out, but it's just got to.

Dick put his hands on my shoulders and looking at me said, "Well, I have to go now. I go back to Ireland tomorrow, so I won't see you again before you leave. Keep me posted as to your schedule. I'll figure out a way to see you wherever you are. Take care, and sweet dreams."

I watched the Jeep slowly disappear into the fog. I wanted to believe that he would write and visit me, but with so many miles separating us, and with all the complications war imposed on us, perhaps I was hoping for too much. I went into the house and fell into bed. But my sleep was fitful, and I tossed and turned all night. I must have re-lived the evening a dozen times in my head.

The next few days will seem like eternity as I wait in hopes for his letter.

"The Five Jovers, 1907" l-r Charles, Rafael, Julian, Lorenzo, Tommy

"The Six Model Maids – 1920" Violet Ella Lines (Nena's mother) 2nd. From left

Above and right:
"The 2 Jovers,"
Rafael and Tommy

"The 2 Jovers" 1920

"The 2 Jovers" 1928

"The 2 Jovers" 1928

Violet Ella Lines — 1920

Photographs

BIRMINGHAM HIPPODROME

5.10 • TWICE NIGHTLY • 7.25
MONDAY, MAY 14th, 1945
MATINEES ON WEDNESDAY, THURSDAY & SATURDAY AT 2.30

Telephone: MIDland 2576-77

Proprietors: THE HAYMARKET CAPITOL LTD.
Joint Managing Directors: MARK OSTRER / L. W. FARROW
DIRECTION: VAL PARNELL
Artistes Booking Control: CISSIE WILLIAMS
Licensee and Manager: BERTIE ADAMS
Press Representative: LAWSON E. TROUT, F.Inst.P.
Musical Director: KEVIN MALLON
(THE GENERAL THEATRE CORPORATION LTD.)

In accordance with the requirements of the Licensing Justices:—
(a) The public may leave at the end of the performance by all exits and entrances other than those used as queue waiting rooms and the doors at such exits and entrances shall at the time be open. (b) All gangways, passages and staircases shall be kept entirely free from chairs or any other obstruction. (c) Persons shall not be permitted to stand or sit in any of the intersecting gangways. If standing be permitted at the rear of the seating sufficient space shall be left for persons to pass easily to and fro. (d) The fireproof curtain shall at all times be maintained in working order and shall be lowered at the beginning of and during the time of every performance.

This Theatre is disinfected throughout with Jeyes' Fluid

PRICES OF ADMISSION
(including Entertainment Tax)
Boxes 22/- and 16/4, Imperial Fauteuils 5/-, Fauteuils 4/-, Stalls 3/-, Grand Circle 4/6, Circle 3/-, Balcony 9d.

NEXT WEEK

THE TWO LESLIES
LESLIE SARONY & LESLIE HOLMES

JUDY SHIRLEY & SAM BROWNE

BILLY CARYLL & HILDA MUNDY

SCOTT & WHALEY

AND FULL VARIETY COMPANY

TOM ARNOLD
presents
(for Whitley Productions Ltd.)

THE

"BIG TOP" CIRCUS

1 OVERTURE

2 LITTLE SYLVIA
   Ballerina on Horseback

3 PRONTOS WATER ACT

4 DUET IN CREAM
   Equine Elegance

5 OLSEN'S AMAZING SEAL
   He will astound you with his Antics

6 THE ROSINAS Thrills of the Air

7 LOU LENNY and her
   UNRIDE-ABLE MULE
   A Yell! A Scream! A Roar!

8 THE LAI FOUNS
   Sensational Chinese Wonders

INTERMISSION

9 YOUNG ROY
   The World's Youngest High School Rider

10 VICTOR JULIAN and his PETS
    Monkeys and Dogs
    The Smallest Comedians in the world

11 TOMMY JOVER, NENA & RAF
    Our Star Clowns

12 MARIORA Rastelli's Successor
    The Wonder Girl Juggler

13 WORLD FAMOUS LIBERTY
    HORSE SEXTET
    A Symphony in Grey
    Presented by Peggy Holt

14 CLOWN ENTREE
    Len and Alby Austin and Billy Merchant ("Doo-doo" and "Little Billy")

15 THE BIG CAGE—
    Tigers and Lions
    Presented by Clem Merk
    Circusdom's Biggest Thrill
    The Ringmaster: Victor Julian

Manager .... Archie Stanton
Stage Director .... Frederick A. Colk
Assistant Stage Manager .. Frederick Walker
Musical Director .... Archie Stanton
(For Tom Arnold's "Big Top" Circus Company)

LIVERPOOL EMPIRE
Commencing MONDAY, APRIL 2nd, 1945
EVENINGS 5.30 AND 7.45
MATINEES on MON. WED. & SAT. at 2.0

CIRCUSDOM'S BIGGEST THRILL!
BIG CAGE LIONS AND TIGERS
TOMMY JOVER NENA & RAF
FOUR STAR CLOWNS
OLSEN'S AMAZING SEAL
TOM ARNOLD'S BIG TOP CIRCUS
LAI FOUNS
VICTOR JULIAN AND HIS PETS MONKEYS & DOGS
WORLD-FAMOUS LIBERTY HORSES
YOUNG ROY WORLD'S YOUNGEST HIGH SCHOOL RIDER
A SYMPHONY IN GREY
LITTLE SYLVIA BALLERINA ON HORSEBACK
MARIORA
LEN and ALBY AUSTIN
LOU LENNY AND HER UNRIDEABLE MULE
COUP'S AMAZING SAMOYEDS
ROSINAS THRILLS OF THE AIR

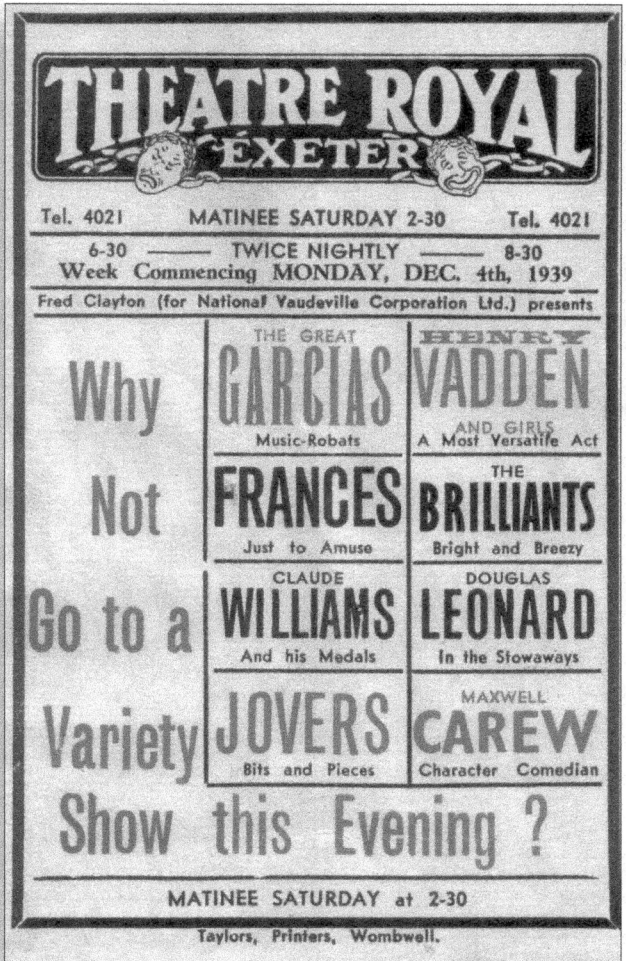

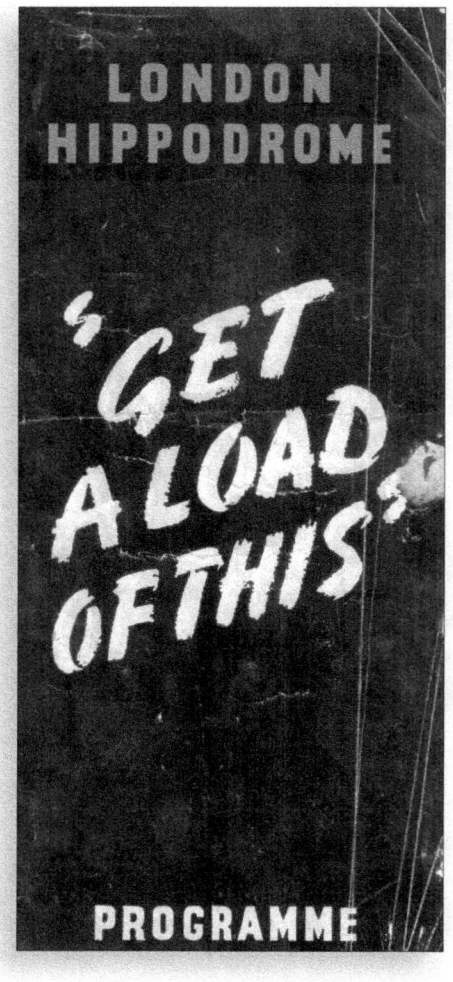

ALL MIRANDA. There's good natured rivalry between Tommy Trinder and Nena Jover (Tommy Jover's daughter) with their respective "take-offs" of Carmen Miranda, the Brazilian bombshell. Tommy is, of course, featuring the impression with the greatest success at the London Palladium where it is voted to be one of the most brilliant things the enterprising comic has done. Nena's "Miranda" is going great guns in George Black's other musical "Get a Load of This," and is proving as big a hit at the Prince of Wales's Theatre as it has already done at the London Hippodrome. Then, the American Forces, and maybe some of our own boys, are to see Carmen Miranda when she shortly visits this country under the American U.S.O. and Overseas Artistes scheme. She may also broadcast.

THE PALLADIUM

Proprietors: **GENERAL THEATRE CORPORATION LIMITED.**

Joint Managing Directors: MARK OSTRER, L. W. FARROW.

Direction ... ... VAL FARNELL.
Artistes Booking Control ... ... CISSIE WILLIAMS.
Resident Manager ... ... DAVID POLLOCK.

GEORGE BLACK'S
MUSICAL FUNFARE
"HAPPY and GLORIOUS"

Produced by
ROBERT NESBITT

Dances arranged by JOAN DAVIS
Musical Adviser: DEBROY SOMERS

PRICES OF ADMISSION (including Entertainments Tax):—
STALLS 13/- 9/8 6/6 4/6
GRAND CIRCLE 7/6 6/- 5/-
UPPER CIRCLE 3/6 2/6
BOXES 26/- 28/6 38/- 39/- 52/-

All Seats Bookable in Advance.
Box Office Open 10 to 9. Phone: Ger. 7373.

In the interest of Public Health this Theatre is disinfected throughout with JEYES FLUID.

THIS THEATRE IS FULLY LICENSED. SMOKING PERMITTED.

In accordance with the requirements of the London County Council.

1.—The Public may leave at the end of the performance or by all exit doors and such doors must at that time be open.
2.—All gangways, corridors, staircases and external passageways intended for exit shall be kept entirely free from obstruction, whether permanent or temporary.
3.—Persons shall not be permitted to stand or sit in any of the gangways intersecting the seating or to sit in any of the other gangways. If standing be permitted in the gangways at the sides and rear of the seating, it shall be limited to the numbers indicated in the notices exhibited in those positions.
4.—The safety curtain must be lowered and raised in the presence of each audience.

For Advertisement Rates, apply to
P. A. CRAMER & CO., LTD., Advertising Contractors,
7ss, Old Compton Street, London, W.1.
'Phone: Gerrard 1404
Printed by PRATT & CO., 4 & 6, Heddon Street,
Regent Street, W.1. 'Phone: Regent 3890.

GEORGE BLACK'S MUSICAL FUNFARE
"HAPPY and GLORIOUS"

1. **FANFARE** (Decor by Doris Zinkeisen)
   The Master of the Music: VICTOR STANDING
   The Mistress of the Rhythm: ZOE GAIL
   THE ARGYLL OCTETTE, THE PALLADIUM GIRLS and THE DANCE BAND
   ('Happy and Glorious Day.' Music by Walter Ridley. Lyric by Syd Colin and Bob Musel)

2. **TRINDER RETURNS**

3. **TOMMY JOVER, NINA, RAF & FE**
   Burlesque in Rhythm

4. **"RHYTHM MAKES THE WORLD GO ROUND"** (Decor by Alec Shanks)
   (Lyrics and Music by Walter Ridley, Bob Musel and Michael Carr)
   The Singer: ELISABETH WELCH
   The North: RENEE GUSCOTT, MARY SCOTT, LOLA DERROL, DIANA GLOVER, CORA VARDELL, LAETITIA MONTFORD
   The East: MARQUEEZ and Ensemble
   The South: JOAN CARROD, ENA CURTIS, ROMA DARRELL
   The West: GEORGE GRAY and Ensemble

5. **WORDS and MUSIC**
   TOMMY TRINDER and ZOE GAIL interrupted by JACK WILLIAMS, ALAN BAILEY, GEORGE WILMER, not to mention TEDDY FINCH and "JOE"

6. **HIGHLAND BRIGADE** (Decor by Stern)
   The Highlanders: THE DAGENHAM GIRL PIPERS
   The Singer: VICTOR STANDING

7. **'THIS IS THE ARMY, Mr. TRINDER'**
   The Officers: ALAN BAILEY and GEORGE WILMER
   The Sergeant: JACK WILLIAMS
   The Batman: TOMMY TRINDER

8. **THE GUARDS BRIGADE**
   ('Marching on Parade.' Lyrics and Music by Michael Carr, Freddie Frisker and John Turner)
   ZOE GAIL AND THE MILITARY BAND
   THE DAGENHAM GIRL DRUMMERS and FULL ENSEMBLE

   INTERMISSION

9. **TAPPING TO THE BATON**
   The Leader of the Band: GEORGE GRAY and THE GIRLS

10. **LEASE-LEND** (Howard Thomas)
    TOMMY TRINDER and ZOE GAIL

11. **ELISABETH WELCH**
    The Sophisticated Lady

12. **TOMMY TRINDER**
    'I Love Good Music.'
    (Lyric and Music by Michael Carr)
    Guitarist—CHAPPIE D'AMATO

13. **'MUSIC, MAESTRO, PLEASE'** (Decor by Doris Zinkeisen)
    DEBROY SOMERS' STAGE ORCHESTRA
    introducing ELISABETH WELCH, ZOE GAIL, GEORGE GRAY and THE PALLADIUM GIRLS

14. **A GUEST ARTISTE**

15. **'HAPPY AND GLORIOUS'**
    (Lyric and Music by Debroy Somers)
    VICTOR STANDING and THE ENTIRE COMPANY

Costumes Designed and Executed by ALEC SHANKS.
Tailoring and Uniforms by MORRIS ANGEL.
Shoes by GAMBA. Masks by HUGH SKILLEN.
CHAPPIE D'AMATO appears by kind permission of the Directors of Hatchetts.
Orchestral Drums used on the Stage by the L. W. HUNT DRUM MANUFACTURING CO.
Scenery Constructed by BRUNSKILL and LOVEDAY and HARRY DELVIN and Painted by ALEC JOHNSTONE and EDWARD DELANY.

Chief of Production Department: CHARLES HENRY.

NENA JOVER  TOMMY JOVER  RAF JOVER

HENDERSON TWINS  DICK (TUBBY) HENDERSON  DICK HENDERSON, Jun.

SUNNY ROGERS with JOAN, JILL and JEAN

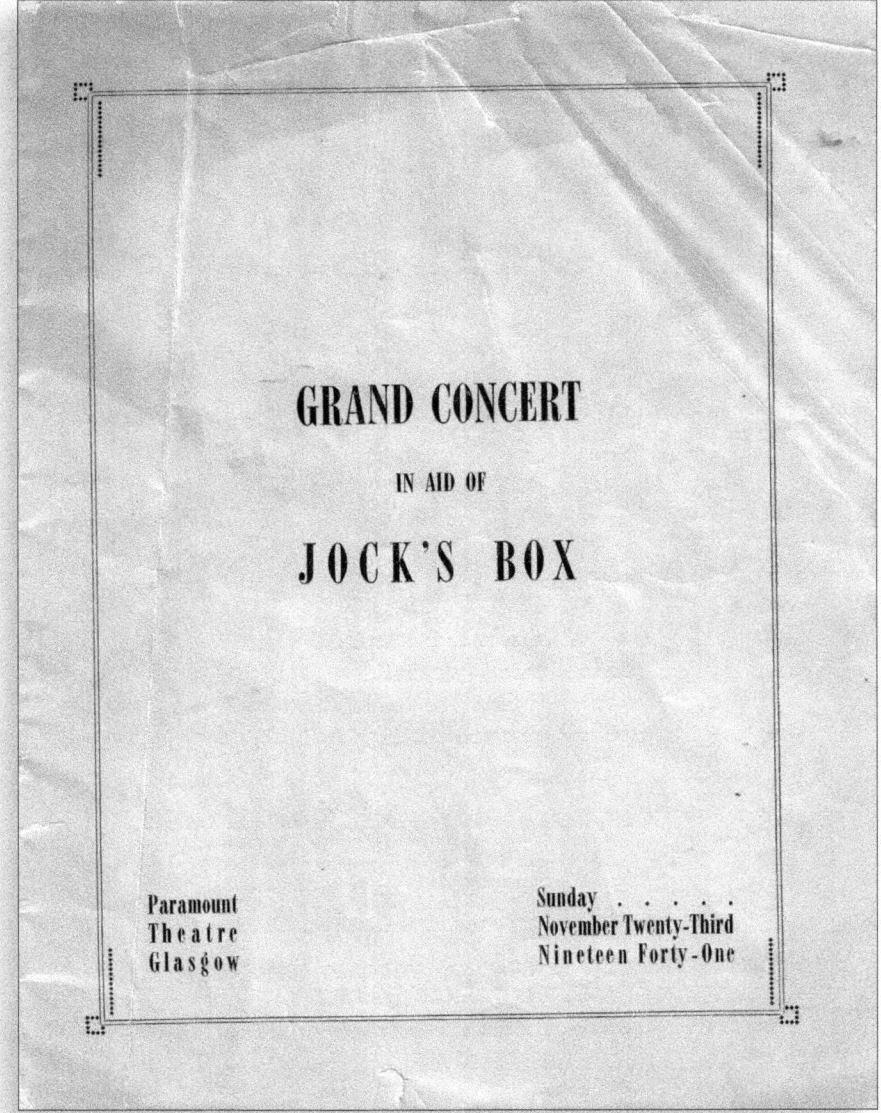

GRAND
ANNUAL
PANTOMIME

Red Riding Hood

W. B. CARR
(Joan B. Carr, F.S.O.A.)
Consulting Optician
1 Bishopton Lane, Stockton-on-Tees
Telephone 66778

FRANK E. FRANKS Presents
The Grand Olde Pantomime

RED RIDING HOOD

Written, Staged and Presented by Frank E. Franks

THE PRINCIPAL CHARACTERS:

IMMORTALS
Fairy Sunshine . . . . . Joan D'Arcy   The Wicked Wolf . . . . . Fred O'Dare

MORTALS
Prince Valiant . . . . . Garcia Owen   Polly Perkins . . . . . M'selle Leonara
Reggie, His Valet . . . . Babs Gordon   Dame Durden
Marjory Dawe . . . . . Nena Jover   Widow Horner . . . . . Tom Cable
Baron Badlot . . . . . Huntley Macdonald   Red Riding Hood . . . . . Dot Carr
Jimmy Green and Johnny Stout . . Raf and Fe   The Woodcutters . . The Royal Breconia Octette
and
SIMPLE SIMON . . . . FRANK E. FRANKS

Supported with Strong Specialities by
TOMMY JOVER with Nena, Raf, and Fe   THE ROYAL BRECONIA OCTETTE
France's Funniest Musical Clowns   Male Voices Extraordinary
M'SELLE LEONARA   LARRY GORDON & BABS
A French Artiste of Repute   America's Greatest Dancing Team
TOM CABLE & DOT CARR   THE THREE PALS
CUMBERLAND & YORKE
The Modern Entertainers
THE 24 EX-SERVICE LOVELIES   THE 16 TINY TAPPERS
AND FULL COMPANY OF 80 FIRST CLASS PANTOMIME ARTISTES

THE SCENES
Scene 1. Ye Old Village Fair   Scene 7. The Heart of the Wood
Scene 2. Road to the Wood   Scene 8. Road Thru' the Wood
Scene 3. Exterior of Dame Durden's House   Scene 9. Outside Widow Horner's Cottage
Scene 4. The Village School   Scene 10. Interior of the Cottage
Scene 5. Road to the Wood   Scene 11. The Baron's Library
Scene 6. The Enchanted Garden   Scene 12. The Victory Parade
INTERVAL

HARDY'S 12-15 HIGH STREET, STOCKTON
(OPPOSITE THIS THEATRE)

2 YEARS TO PAY
FULL RANGE OF **UTILITY** FURNITURE ALWAYS ON VIEW
SPLENDID SELECTION OF SECOND-HAND **FURNITURE** AND PIANOS

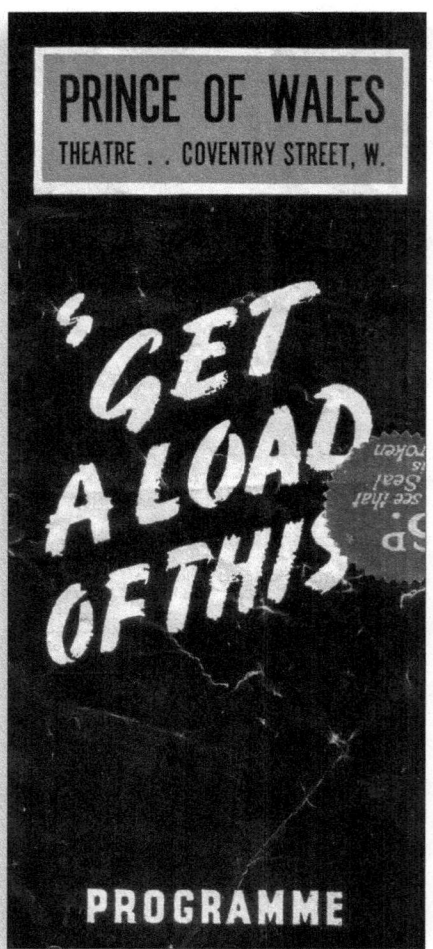

Chapter Twenty

The first thing I did when we got to the Hippodrome Theatre in Brighton was ask the stage doorman if there was a letter for Jover.

"Just a minute, luv. I haven't checked the post yet."

I walked through to the stage. The conductor had just finished rehearsing my friends, the Henderson Twins. I greeted them and promised to see them later.

I handed our music to the conductor and introduced myself and the act, "Tommy Jover, with Nena and Julian. I'm Nena. You're Gerald Hathaway?"

"Yes. Please call me Gerald. We won't be needing these," he said as he handed me back a stack of music. We'll just need parts for piano, drums, violin, saxophone and cello." I looked down into the pit. It wasn't like the Palladium orchestra or even the one at Blackpool, but was typical of Music Halls during the war. All the young men were off fighting. These men were older, but they were good musicians who did their best under the circumstances.

Gerald tapped his baton on the light over his podium. "Gentlemen. We'll now rehearse Tommy Jover, Nena and Julian. We open with 'Rhapsody in Blue.'" He turned to me, "You play sixteen bars, right?"

"Yes. Then I pick a violin off the piano and walk downstage. Gradually fade the music, then stop when my dad, Tommy, walks onstage and joins me. We exchange some patter. He asks me, 'Do you mind if I smoke?' 'I don't care if you burn.' At that point, my dad reaches over and breaks my violin with a prop knife. 'You want a rim shot for that, huh?' Yes, that's the cue for my exit music. Julian then enters with his guitar. Tommy joins him with his concertina. They play some music, do some patter and do various sight gags. Your next cue is … 'and one more thing'.…"

"That's when you do the Carmen Miranda impersonation?"

"Yes, I'd like that intro to be really loud and lively."

They played the intro and one chorus as I mimed the words. It was a little slow, so I asked Gerald if he would pick up the tempo a little. Just then, out of the corner of my eye, I could see my dad coming. He had been running and was out of breath.

"Sorry I'm late. How far have you got?"

"We just finished 'I, yi, yi, yi.' I have a million things to do, so I'll run along. See you later." I left him to rehearse the music for Julian's tap dance, the tango that my brother and I did, and finally the burlesque dance he did with Julian.

I rushed back to the stage door and checked the J box. There was a letter, and it was from him! I tore up to my dressing room and shut the door. It was a real letter, not something he'd tossed off in a couple of minutes. He told me all about Langford Lodge, the Lockheed base where he was stationed, and the beautiful lake nearby he was unable to reach because of the thicket of rhododendrons surrounding it. He said he was tired and hungry, and how are you, and when exactly are you going to be in Liverpool? He told me he had nine days of vacation coming up and that he and Charlie had already made plans to visit Scotland. The ferry from Ireland docked in Liverpool, and if I were there at that time, he would come and see me. As it happened, our letters crossed, and he arrived in Liverpool the day after I left. So, he went north to Scotland, and I went south to London.

Over the next few months, we exchanged many long letters. Sometimes, Dick was able to visit me for half a day or an evening. Those times were precious and often a complete surprise. Once he tracked me down in Huddersfield, an industrial city in northern England. He had an overnight pass, but Mrs. Norton, our landlady, had no extra room for him – not even a couch. Determined to accommodate him somehow, she gathered up some blankets and pillows and let him sleep in the bathtub. Lucky for him, it was a typical large English tub. Appreciating her efforts, Dick thanked her and began to relate some of his experiences as an American in the U.K.

"Mrs. Norton, do you know what the clerk at the hotel in Manchester asked me after I had registered?"

"Ee, I've no idea."

"She said, 'Sir, what time would you like to be knocked up in the morning?'"

"So?"

"Well, in America, being knocked up is the slang way of saying you're pregnant."

She laughed and in her strong Yorkshire accent said, "Bah gum! That's a goodun I can't wait to tell that to me oosband." The next morning, dear Mrs. Norton, thrilled with the romance blooming under her roof, dug into her reserves and served Dick a wonderful breakfast. The word got out somehow about her foreign guest, and as he ate various neighbors kept dropping in to catch a glimpse of the Yank who had slept in Mrs. Norton's bathtub.

We hadn't had an opportunity to be alone much during this brief visit, so Dick said, "Let's go a little early to the railway station. I have something I want to tell you."

He said his goodbyes to everyone, and we started to walk. He took my hand and said, "My contract with Lockheed ends in a month. They've offered me a job in Africa on a base yet to be built. We'd be modifying planes for desert warfare."

"Oh, no! Africa! I'll never see you if you go to Africa!" I said, getting very upset.

"Wait a minute. Wait a minute. I didn't say I'd accepted."

"Well, does that mean you'll go back to America?"

"No. I'm not doing that either."

Dick loved to tease, but the suspense was killing me.

"Well, what are you going to do?"

"I'm going to try to join the U.S. Navy. I go to Londonderry next week. I don't know if I'll pass the physical because of my eye, but if they accept me I'm told they'll probably assign me to some place in England."

"Oh! That would be wonderful!" I hardly dared hope that would happen. "That's even better than being stationed in Ireland with Lockheed."

I flung my arms around him and gave him a big hug. If hopes and wishes had any effect, his acceptance into the U.S. Navy was assured. We arrived at the station and went into the waiting room. I didn't want to ask what he'd do if the Navy didn't accept him. I thought he'd probably go back to America. If that happened, who knows? He might change his mind or meet someone else. We were both wrapped up in our individual thoughts when the train's whistle brought us back to the moment. We walked out on the platform. Before getting on the train, Dick lifted my chin up and said, "Look. I'm going to do anything I can to stay in England. I'll let you know what's happening."

He got on the train, and I waved until it was out of sight.

Chapter Twenty-One

Dick was always curious about my daily life. It was so different from his. Some events even surprised me. One happened in West Hartlepool, a dreary mining town. After the act one evening, the stage manager pulled me aside and said, "There's a man in my office who says he'll buy a war bond for every girl in the show who kisses him."

"Oh! Who is he? What does he look like?"

"He's the butcher, a little on the pudgy side."

I didn't relish kissing a complete stranger no matter how great the cause, but my friend Zena standing next to me said, "Look, we can't not do it. Let's get there first, so we don't have to kiss him after ten other girls."

"Good idea. Let's go."

We raced to the office, startling the man who may have misinterpreted our eagerness, kissed him and fled.

"Oh, what I do for England!" said Zena.

Another time, we were playing the Finsbury Park Empire Theatre in London. Headlining the bill was Teddy Brown who was brilliant on the Xylophone. He was literally a big American star, weighing almost 300 pounds. He wowed the audience as he casually walked up to the instrument and, with what looked like minimum effort, produced wonderful music. I had only a nodding acquaintance with him, so I was surprised when he sent me a message: "Would you please come to Mr. Brown's dressing room. There's someone he'd like you to meet."

Not knowing what to expect, but curious, I went and knocked on the door.

"Come in!"

I opened the door and came face to face with Douglas Fairbanks, Jr. I almost fainted and immediately noted that he was shorter than I thought he'd be and was wearing a uniform of an officer in the Commandos. He seemed very shy. Teddy introduced us.

"I'm very happy to meet you," I said.

"Nice to meet you, too," he answered.

I turned to Teddy, expecting him to explain a little more about why he had sent for me, but he didn't say a word. He kept looking first at Fairbanks, then at me. I began to get very uncomfortable. What's this all about? Is this just to give me the thrill of meeting a movie star, or is he trying to fix me up? All I knew was that I'd rather be somewhere else, so I said, "So nice to meet you. Sorry I have to run. G'bye, Teddy!" and I left. I'll never know who was more relieved at my departure – Fairbanks or I.

Some of the stories I told Dick were really other people's adventures. I wrote and told him about Koringa, a lady who billed herself as "The Female Kafir." She usually worked in circuses, but there weren't many of those around at the time, so she was happy to be working anywhere. The animals she worked with – alligators and pythons – did not always cooperate. One night, one of her alligators slid over the footlights into the orchestra pit. You never saw such a scramble as the musicians crawled over each other, abandoning their instruments in a desperate attempt to get away. On another occasion, Koringa was beside herself – her python refused to work. He just wanted to sleep.

"Can't you just wake him up?" asked the manager.

"No, he's eaten, and he needs a month to digest his meal."

We all looked at the python. Sure enough, he had a big bulge in his middle.

"Well, why did you feed him?"

"I didn't. He helped himself. He ate the theatre cat."

We were all dismayed, having grown quite fond of Ginger.

Chapter Twenty-Two

I waited two long weeks with fingers crossed before I heard the result of Dick's trip to Londonderry. Finally, his letter arrived with the news – he was in the U.S. Navy! "I didn't pass the eye test," he wrote, "but they accepted me anyway. I am now an Aviation Machinist Mate Second Class."

He added he was disappointed that the Navy didn't take advantage of his skills and experience with aircraft. He'd have an office job. He'd know more after he arrived at his base which would be in a tiny village near the town of Exeter in Devonshire in the southern part of England.

I was thrilled. Perhaps now there would be a chance of our meeting more often. I looked at the map and noticed that the cathedral city of Salisbury was about half way between Wimbledon and Exeter, less than a two-hour train ride from home. Perhaps we could meet there. I could go there and still get back in time for the show, and if Dick could get enough time off to meet me that would be wonderful. Dick thought it was a great idea, and he was sure he could work things out. In the Navy, his free time would be more limited than when he was with Lockheed, but at least now we were in the same country.

The first opportunity to meet came sooner than expected. The show I was in was booked at Wimbledon Theatre, and Dick phoned to say he could get away from the base for a few hours. At the station, the ticket master couldn't understand why I was going so far only to come back the same day. I didn't explain but took my ticket and walked to the platform, trying to ignore the government poster that asked, "Is this trip really necessary?" Dick met me at the station. He looked handsome in his uniform and so happy to see me.

As we stood on the platform and with his arms still around me, Dick took the moment to propose – sort of. He said, "When are we going to get married?"

Before I could answer, he added, "We should wait until the war is over. Either one of us might get killed, and if we did get married now it would be harder to be apart."

I didn't know what to say. I wasn't upset that he didn't get on bended knee to ask me. The way he said it was an acknowledgement of how we felt about each other. But it was difficult to answer, because there really wasn't a question. I didn't want to enter into a hasty war marriage either and was grateful he was being so sensible. All I could do was nod as I choked back my emotions.

"Look," he said, as he kissed me. "We can get engaged. Waiting will be a good test for us."

I agreed. I had to keep working. It wouldn't be fair to my dad to leave the act without lots of warning. And anyway, if I didn't work, the government would get interested in my case. Then my life would get even more complicated. Dick broke into my thoughts, "Let's go see the cathedral."

"Yes, let's. I've never seen it before. Let's go."

He took my hand, and we walked out of the station and on into the town. As the cathedral came into view, Dick drew out his camera and took a picture.

"This is so beautiful," he said. "Let's sit on that bench over there before we go in."

We sat down. Dick had a very serious look on his face. He put his

Chapter Twenty-Two

hand in his pocket and drew out a little box and gave it to me without saying anything.

"What's this?"

"You'll never know unless you open it."

I opened it and gasped. It was a beautiful ring with two big diamonds.

"Oh, my gosh! It's gorgeous! It's so big!"

"I wanted it big enough to warn the other guys off," he said, as he put it on my finger. I never expected anything so lavish.

"When did you get this?"

"I bought it in Ireland."

"Oh. You were pretty sure of me, weren't you?"

"Well, have you changed your mind?"

"Are you kidding? Just try to get away from me."

And with that, I fell into his arms. We were lost in our own little world, kissing and whispering sweet nothings to each other, when we suddenly realized we had an audience. I glanced over to the pathway. There stood a group of schoolgirls in uniform, pointing at us and giggling. They giggled even louder when Dick gave them a big grin and said, "Hi! How are ya doing?"

They stifled their giggles when their teacher appeared and said, "Come along, girls!" They followed her into the cathedral.

After a few minutes, we went in too. We didn't stay long. Every time we turned a corner, there they were. One look at us sent them off into more fits of giggles. For their teacher's peace of mind, we thought we'd better leave.

All too soon, it was time to catch the train back to Wimbledon.

"When can we do this again?" Dick asked. "This is a great place to meet."

"I'll have to check our dates. I think we'll be back in London in a couple of weeks. Is there some way I can phone you?"

"No. They won't let us accept phone calls. We'll have to plan ahead. I could always phone you."

"OK. I'll write as soon as I'm sure of the dates."

We walked back to the station and stood on the platform where my train would arrive – a scene we were to repeat many times. Now that I was engaged, it felt like my life had taken on a very serious turn. I didn't expect any adverse reaction from my family but wondered what Dick's would have to say about his commitment to a girl who lived so far away. Dick gave me a big hug as the train pulled in. "Love you. Keep those letters coming," he said as he gave me a kiss. I kissed him back and got on the train. As the train left, I waved with my left hand, flashing my new ring.

Chapter Twenty-Three

Wimbledon was in the middle of an air raid when I got back. I hurried down Queens Road for the 10-minute walk to my house, diving into the bushes every time a bomb sounded close. My parents were relieved that I'd got back safely and wanted to know all about my trip. I gave them the news and showed them my ring. Everyone gathered around. "It's beautiful!" said Fe. They were all happy for me. "Dick seems like a very nice man," my dad said. "You should write a letter to his mother. Maybe send her a little gift."

All of a sudden I realized that marriage wasn't something that affects just two people; in our case, it would be two extended families 7,000 miles apart. I wondered what I could find as a little gift for Dick's mother. There was nothing in the shops. The only possibility was something from an antique shop. As I pondered all this, my dad was getting anxious.

He said, "We'd better get going. We have a show to do. I wonder how many people will want to go out in this air raid just to see us."

It always amazed me that people would leave the relative comfort of their homes to take their chances in the streets, then sit calmly in a theatre and laugh and applaud our efforts.

After the Blitz in 1940, the bombing continued but not at such a heavy, continuous rate. Now in January 1944, it started up again with a vengeance. The raids were no longer limited to nighttime, which made life much more difficult for everyone.

June 12, 1944 arrived with a new threat – the V1 buzz bomb, or Doodlebug (named after a New Zealand insect). This was an unmanned flying bomb. It flew low, and its engine emitted a loud, ominous drone. Strange as it sounds, everyone felt safe as long as they could hear that noise. The minute the engine cut off, everyone ducked for cover because, having lost its momentum, the bomb just dropped. It was not guided in any way. This type of bomb did not go deep but caused immense damage over a wide area. Clever, brave RAF pilots learned that by carefully maneuvering their wings under a bomb, they could tip it over so that it fell harmlessly into the English Channel. I was surprised to learn after the war that out of 6,725 Doodlebugs aimed toward British shores, the RAF destroyed 3,500 of them with their tipping technique. The next of Hitler's "secret weapons" was the V2 rocket. It flew faster than the speed of sound. There was simply no defense against it.

During these heavy raids, my sister Fe and I slept in the Morrison shelter my dad had erected in the sitting room. It was a new type of protection from bombs the government had issued. This contraption was about two feet tall and six feet square. It had a sturdy leg at each corner. The top was a big sheet of iron. The sides were wire mesh. The rest of the family was scattered in different rooms around the house. We all took reasonable precautions during air raids but had become fatalists, thinking if a bomb had your name on it there wasn't anything you could do to avoid it.

There was one night that had been particularly rough. We'd dressed warmly as all our windows had been blown out again. It was hard to sleep. Apart from the fear of being killed by a bomb, the deafening noise from the ack-ack (anti-aircraft) guns mounted on the Wimbledon railway tracks put any thought of sleep out of our minds.

To distract from the horrors of the moment, I tried to think of happier times when I was a young girl living in that little house in Mitcham. It had been a magnet for all the children in the neighborhood, mostly because of all the crazy costumes, wigs and props my dad let us play with. They were left over from all the shows and pantomimes he had performed in.

What fun it was to pretend to be a Chinese coolie with a baldhead and pigtail or even a pirate with a wooden leg. My favorite outfit was a silver wig with a big bun over each ear and a big tulle skirt. I must have looked ridiculous, but I felt like a beautiful ballerina as I pranced around. We'd play for hours in our fantasy world, coming down to earth only when we heard our mother call, "Dinner's ready!"

And then there was the day my mother made a big batch of soup in her new pressure cooker. She put the pot on the dining room table and carefully released the pressure valve. What happened next was like a scene in a slapstick comedy routine. A geyser shot up to the ceiling and came down, covering all of us in a milky liquid. We ran around with our soup plates, screaming with laughter, as we tried to catch the liquid and minimize the disaster. I can't remember what we had for supper, but it certainly wasn't soup.

And the time my dad crawled up into the attic to fetch something. There was no floor, and he had to walk carefully, straddling the joists. Suddenly, much to the surprise of the rest of us sitting at the table in the dining room, my dad's leg came crashing through the ceiling. He came downstairs nursing some deep scratches, looked up at the ceiling and said he had to leave for the theatre. Nobody seemed to know what to do about this unexpected remodel. Raf couldn't resist having fun with it. He found an old pair of pants, cut one leg off, tied a shoe to the bottom and pushed it through the hole. That pant leg with the shoe was a great conversation piece for visitors for weeks until our mother couldn't stand it any longer and had someone fix the hole.

There always seemed to be something to laugh about growing up in our home. I was trying to think of other adventures, but I must have dozed off, as the next thing I remember was Fe's hand over my mouth and her voice whispering in my ear, "There's a man walking around the house!"

With broken glass everywhere, we could hear the crunch as he walked around. Now he was in our room! Only the lower part of his legs was visible. We clung to each other, too scared to say anything and too scared to move. Suddenly, we heard a shout, "Is anybody home?"

It was Dick! In my excitement, I forgot where I was and sat up, banging my head on the top of the shelter, almost knocking myself out.

"Hello, Dick!" my sister yelled.

"Where are you?"

"We're under here!"

He squatted down, looked in at us and burst out laughing.

"What is this, a nest? You two look a sight!"

We crawled out on our hands and knees in our flannel pajamas, wool hats and mittens. My forehead was hurting. I look my hat off and could feel a big, tender lump forming.

"Oh!" I groaned. "You didn't tell me you were coming."

"Well, I have a two-day pass. I ran to the station. There wasn't time to make a phone call. What happened to your head?"

"It's your fault. When I heard your voice, I sat up and banged it on the shelter."

"Poor baby! Come over here. I'll kiss it and make it better."

Snuggled up in his lap, everything looked better. Hearing voices, the rest of the family started to appear. They were surprised and happy to see Dick. My little brother Richard jumped up and down. He was so excited – his supply of chewing gum was about to be replenished.

"What a night," said my mother. "Those bombs were really close. Has anyone listened to the news?"

Nobody had, so Fe turned on the radio. The BBC announcer was giving an account of the night's air raid. He mentioned the East End Docks, hit once again. There can't be anything left there to bomb, I thought. Then he went on to report on the buzz bombs – how many the RAF had destroyed, how many got through and where they landed. Our jaws dropped when he said that an elementary school in Wimbledon had been obliterated. "Gosh! There's an elementary school just around the corner," said my mother. "Do you suppose it could be that one?"

"I wouldn't be surprised," said my dad. "Something big exploded near us."

"We were so lucky," said Mummy. "I don't know about anyone else, but I could do with a cup of tea. And if someone will clean up the glass in the kitchen, we can have some breakfast."

Dick and Julian volunteered, while Fe and I ran off to get dressed. When we came back, we all pitched in, making toast and stirring the oatmeal. After we'd eaten, Dick said, "Let's go and see if that's the school that was bombed."

Four of us went. As we turned the corner, we stopped, speechless. There was nothing left of the school. Some houses facing it had lost their front walls. None had any windows left.

"Thank goodness this happened at night," I said. "Just imagine how many children would have been killed if the bomb had hit in the daytime."

"Hey, you guys," said Dick. "Do you realize how close that bomb came to your house? Those houses facing the school back up to your property."

I knew only too well how close the bombs had come. The Morrison shelter gave me a certain sense of security, but I kept imagining the house collapsing and having to be dug out. How would the rescuers know Fe and I were there, how many hours would it take, and would we have enough air to last? Then a macabre thought – what if that sheet of iron under a ton of bricks squashed us flat? My imagination was running wild. I had to think of something else. It was a miracle to all of us that our brick house, built in 1895, had been able to withstand so many close bomb blasts. We walked home, grateful to have one to go to, even if it was in a mess.

Dick came with us to the theatre in Golders Green that evening. Fe also came along. Someday she'd replace me in the act, and my dad thought it would be a good idea if she watched me whenever possible.

I couldn't understand why my dressing room was so cold.

"Well, look up there," Fe said. "No wonder!"

"Gosh!" There was a hole about six inches square open to the sky in the ceiling. It was too high up for us to stuff anything in it. I shrugged my shoulders. There was nothing anyone could do about it right now.

"At least it isn't raining," I said and got ready for the show.

Dick wandered around backstage while we worked. Things we thought of as the norm, he found fascinating. He could hardly contain himself as he told us of what he'd just seen. We were on the bill with Kardoma, a magician, whose billing read "Fills the Stage with Flags." Almost every trick he did involved flags. They appeared out of hats, his sleeves and pockets, vases, etc. By the end of his act, every corner of the stage was filled with Union Jacks of all sizes. Passing by his dressing room, Dick happened to glance in and was amazed to see Kardoma's wife folding each flag into tiny squares in readiness for the next performance.

"It must take her hours to do that, and her husband undoes it in ten minutes," Dick said in amazement. "And she does this twice every evening!"

"Well, somebody has to do it."

"Yes, but he's having all the fun. She has the drudgery."

It did sound unfair, but who knew how their arrangement had come about. On tour, we divided our chores – my dad got the work and arranged for our digs, my brother took care of the baggage and talked to the electrician about lighting for the act. Whoever was available took band rehearsal. I was left with the traditional chores of a female – grocery shopping and laundry. I did my part willingly until Raf complained once too often about the way I ironed his shirts. I resigned from the laundry business. It was difficult enough trying to find food in a strange town every week without hearing complaints about my ironing skills. Raf wasn't too upset over the loss of his laundress and managed to find a professional to replace me.

After the show in Golders Green, we all got on the underground and went home. My mother was in bed, but she had left us a hot meal and fixed Dick up with a bed. The house was still a mess, but my dad had tacked linoleum over the broken windows, so at least it wasn't freezing inside. I didn't think Dick had a very exciting time with his two-day pass, but he seemed happy. The next morning after breakfast, he said to my mother, "I have to go now. Thank you so much for your warm hospitality. I really feel like one of the family."

"Not at all. You are one of the family. Even if Nena's not here, please come and visit us."

"Thanks. I appreciate that, but whenever I get any free time, I'll be chasing after your daughter wherever she is."

She laughed and gave him a peck on the cheek. "I understand. Have a safe trip back."

As Dick and I walked to the station, he said, "Is there time before my train for you to show me that horse you told me about – you know, the one that helps other horses pull their carts up the hill?"

"Yes, there's time. It's right near the station. But I can't promise you'll see anything."

Dick was referring to a big draft horse, based at the bottom of Wimbledon Hill. It was for hire to help any horse unable to pull its heavily loaded cart up the hill. We were in luck. When we reached the station, we could see the owner of the draft horse hitching him up in front of another horse. At a signal, the draft horse strained to pull its heavy load. He scrambled a bit, and sparks flew from his shoes as he tried to get traction on the cobblestones. We held our breath as we watched the struggle. He was finally successful, and the two horses slowly pulled the cart to the top of the hill.

"Damn!" said Dick. "I wouldn't have missed this for anything. This is something out of the Middle Ages!"

It seemed quaint to me, too, but I knew if not for the war the horse and cart would have disappeared long ago. We went into the station and found the right platform. The sirens were wailing, but the train chugged into the station right on time.

"Is it easy for you to get to Portsmouth? I think we have a date coming up there," I said.

"Is that in England?" he said with a grin. "Just tell me when."

Just before he got on the train, he gave me a big hug and such a long kiss that I was gasping for breath.

"That'll have to last you 'til next time," he said, and with that he was gone.

Chapter Twenty-Four

At the beginning of 1944, we had to address another problem – Julian would be drafted when he turned 18 in April, and there was no younger brother to take his place. Richard was only ten. For the first time, we would have to look beyond the family for a replacement.

Dad spread the word around the business that he was looking for someone to take Julian's place. There was no lack of applicants as the act was now well-established with a good reputation. He interviewed several men, finally settling on Teddy Wimpress. Teddy was in his 30s, could dance, play the guitar a little and knew how to deliver lines. He was nice-looking, though not as tall or striking as my brothers. He was pleasant and conscientious about learning his new role. Julian set about teaching him all the fine points he needed to know.

In the meantime, Julian was dealing with his own problems. He wrote to the government asking for the exact date he would be inducted; Teddy needed to know when he would be joining the act. Two weeks later, he received a confusing reply. The letter stated that as his father was not a British Subject (untrue) Julian had dual citizenship and would at the age of 21 have to declare either Spanish or British citizenship. It asked, "What are your intentions?" The letter went on to say that, if he chose Spanish, he would be treated as a member of an unfriendly country and might be interned. If he chose British, he would be called up for the army. Faced with the inevitable hassle as he tried to straighten out the mess, he wrote back to the government and simply said, "I choose to be British." He wondered why Raf was able to serve in the Royal Marines without any trouble and why things were so difficult for him. His decision prompted another letter from the government stating that his name had been placed in a ballot and that he would not be serving in the army after all but would be working in a coal mine. Julian was to be one of "Bevin's Boys."

Winston Churchill had appointed Ernest Bevin, a strong Labor leader, as Minister of Labor and National Service. The Emergency Powers Act gave him complete control over the labor force and the allocation of manpower. He took his role seriously and became a virtual dictator in this position. Unfortunately, in his zeal to supply the army with enough soldiers, he failed to pay enough attention to the effect the draft would have on coal mines. Private homes and industry were suffering from shortages. Ernest Bevin solved this problem by conscripting 48,000 draftees, about 10% of available men, to fill the desperate need for miners.

Julian was sent to Easington Colliery, a mining village on the northeast coast, for four weeks' training which was almost equally divided into classroom lectures, surface work, physical training and working underground. He was joined by five other young men who were in the same position. They all experienced a huge culture shock as they saw for the first time how coal miners lived and under what conditions they worked. The miners and their families lived in small row houses which they rented from the colliery owners. This made them completely dependent on the only source of employment in the town. "You lose your job, you lose your house," they were told. The community did not hide its resentment for the Tory government or anyone living farther south.

To say that Julian's transition from footlights to coal mines was a shock is a monumental understatement. He says, "The memory of my first trip into a coal mine will always remain with me. The six of us showed up at the mine and stepped into the cage. It seemed to drop at the speed of light to the bottom of the shaft one mile below. We shuffled along ever diminishing tunnels until we were walking almost doubled over. We arrived at a gallery where about a dozen men were drilling blast holes in a bank. Others sprayed water to reduce the dust. Everyone was soaking wet, covered in coal dust and standing in ankle-deep water. The miners stopped their drilling and stared in amazement at the sight of us – six clean, young men. We stared back, realizing with dismay that this was what was in store for us. Suddenly, an older man grabbed my jacket and, pulling me toward him, growled, "You tell 'em, sonny! Tell 'em in London what it's like. Make sure you tell 'em!"

After his training was complete, Julian was assigned to a colliery at Seaham Harbour a few miles away. He was paid three pounds a week and housed in a primitive army-style barracks. Room and board cost him 35 shillings, more than half of what he earned. He was issued a safety helmet, a pair of overalls, steel-capped boots, a safety lamp, a water bottle and a snap tin for sandwiches. The mine was two miles down, then two miles out under the North Sea. His job was to connect and disconnect coal tubs and send them to the surface. Conditions were even worse than he had anticipated. There were no toilet facilities, and the stench was nauseating. Every day brought its share of cuts and bruises. Some mines had showers at the pit head, but Seaham did not. For all his hatred of working in the mines, Julian knew that the pit ponies had it even worse. Some were housed for life underground. The only time they came up to the surface was at Christmas when the mines were closed for a week. Their eyes had to be bandaged as they could not tolerate daylight.

Any other job in the world had to be better than this, he thought. After a year, the day arrived when he decided he couldn't stand it any longer. Not caring about the consequences, he wrote to the authorities telling them so. Nothing could be worse than this, he thought. He did offer to serve the rest of his time in the army, and much to his amazement they agreed to allow him to transfer, probably because the war in Europe was winding down. He was sent to Bally Mena in Northern Ireland where he was taught how to shoot a rifle, throw a hand grenade, march backwards and forwards and how to salute. Someone decided he should join the crack Irish unit, The Ulster Rifles. After several more months of shooting, marching, throwing and saluting, he was transferred to the Royal Army Pay Corps in Aldershot, which being in the south of England gave him the opportunity to come home more frequently. One sad aspect of boys who were conscripted to work in the coal mines concerned the fact that they were not issued a uniform. They were often challenged by members of the public who wrongfully assumed they were avoiding duty in the armed services. "Why is a young, healthy boy like you not in the army?" they wanted to know.

Chapter Twenty-Five

Our next engagement, and our first with Teddy in the act, was in Birmingham in the Midlands. Teddy proved to be an excellent choice. He was a fine straight man for my dad, and they became good friends. His tap dancing was not strong enough, however, and so once again I found myself doing that routine. I now had three quick changes of costumes.

I was happy to see that my friend, Zena Dell, was on the bill with us. She did a song-and-dance act. I always admired the way she sang, while dressed in a man's tuxedo, "I'm Going to Get Lit Up When the Lights Go on in London." She was petite and sang in a debonair, slightly inebriated manner which was very effective. As soon as she saw me, she shouted, "Hey, Nena! I heard from Reggie. He's still getting your cigarettes!"

"Oh, great! It's good to know the system works." I had sent cigarettes through the Red Cross to her husband Reggie who was a prisoner of war in Germany. He was a rear gunner in the RAF and had been shot down during a mission.

A year ago in a letter to Zena, he told her that cigarettes were the currency for buying anything in the camp, either from other prisoners or even the guards. As I filled out the Red Cross form in the tobacco and newspaper shop in Wimbledon, I hoped that Germany was observing the Geneva Convention and that the cigarettes would arrive. With news of success, I repeated my cigarette venture several times, never quite getting over the fact that my giftee was a prisoner of war in an enemy camp in Germany and that somehow the conflict had been set aside temporarily to allow someone to do something nice for another person.

I wondered how much longer Reggie would be a prisoner. The Red Army had fought its way into Poland, Austria and finally Germany's capitol, Berlin. On April 30, 1945, Hitler, realizing the end was near and not wanting to be captured by the Russians, committed suicide along with his wife, Eva Braun, in the chancellery bunker. Only two days before, Italian partisans had captured Il Duce (Mussolini) as he was trying to escape disguised as an army private. He and his mistress, Clara Petacci, were shot and killed near Lake Como. Their bodies were transported to an Esso gasoline station in the Piazzale Loreto in Milan. There, the partisans strung them up by the feet with piano wire. After being buried and dug up twice, Il Duce was finally laid to rest in the family plot in Predappio. On May 4, German forces in northwest Germany, Denmark and Holland surrendered to Field Marshall Montgomery on Luneburg Heath. Hitler's successor, Admiral Donitz, tried to surrender to the Western Forces while still fighting the Russians. His wishes were denied, and he surrendered to the Russians on May 7.

On May 8, 1945, V.E. Day (Victory in Europe Day) was celebrated all over Europe. Britons could hardly believe their long travail was over. However, the war in the Pacific was not yet finished. It continued until August 14 when Japan surrendered after America dropped atom bombs on Hiroshima and Nagasaki. Victory Over Japan (V.J. Day) was celebrated and World War II finally ended.

We were in Leeds when the war in Europe was over. There were no big celebrations. There was still all that unfinished business in the Pacific, and people were tired. It was a huge relief not to have to worry about

Chapter Twenty-Five

what menace might come down from the sky, but sons, husbands and fathers had not yet returned from duty, and what kind of future did they have to look forward to, anyway? England was broke. The war had taken a huge human and monetary toll on its people. Lives needed to be rebuilt as much as buildings.

I had an unexpected visitor when we were working in Birmingham – Dickie Henderson. He had tracked me down to my digs. I hadn't seen him for a couple of years and wondered why he had suddenly decided to look me up. He was wearing an army officer's uniform and didn't waste any time getting to the reason for his visit. He begged me not to marry this American he'd heard I was engaged to.

"I used to stand in front of the Hippodrome Theatre in London and look at your photographs."

"Why on earth didn't you come to the stage door?"

It wasn't as if I had any lingering romantic feelings for him, but I would have liked to have seen him. I couldn't help but think of that old cliché – "Faint heart never won fair lady." I told him I was sorry, but my mind was made up, and I was going ahead with my plans. He left looking sad, and I felt badly about hurting him.

Later that week, an offer arrived for a show from entrepreneur Tom Arnold. It was to be called *Big Top*, and the theme was the circus.

"I thought I'd left the circus behind forever," said my dad, "but the money's good, and Tom Arnold always puts on a good show. Let's do it." And with that, he signed the contract.

Mixing music hall acts with animal acts on a stage seemed strange. I was used to working with the odd dog act, but now all our fellow performers were to be horses, elephants, tigers and who knew what else.

The show opened at the Palace Theatre in Manchester. The animal acts, working in a strange venue, had to make many adjustments. Things didn't always go smoothly. For instance, one night I opened the act and was standing by the footlights waiting for my dad to make his entrance. Unbeknownst to me, when he got to the wings, he found a horse standing in his way. He gave its rear end a gentle push and was horrified when the horse lost its footing on the slippery floor and went down with a crash, pulling curtains and flats with it. Not knowing about any of this, only that there was a terrible noise and that my dad didn't make his entrance on time, I was at a loss as to what to do. I couldn't play the violin I was holding, even if it hadn't been a prop. It was not my instrument. I started to tell the audience about the Chopin Etude I was about to play, hoping and praying that my dad would show up any second. He suddenly fell onto the stage and kept rolling, getting a big laugh from the audience. They probably thought this was part of the act and that he did that in every show.

The tigers were kept in cages backstage, but the elephants and horses needed stables and other quarters in which to spend the night. The trainers were instructed to arrive at the theatre with their animals before the show started so that they could enter through the huge doors at the back of the stage, the same ones used for scenery and large equipment. Once the show started, the doors would be closed and a curtain drawn across, forming the backdrop for the scene.

One evening, there was consternation backstage when it was time for the show to start. Where is the elephant? The stage manager was angry and said, "We can't wait any longer. We'll do the show without it."

He rearranged the program a little, and we all went back to our dressing rooms. Mine was on the ground floor. I started to put on my make-up when I noticed that the lamps on the wall were shaking. Then the wall itself shook. I ran to the door and opened it to see what was happening.

"Shut the door! Shut the door!" a man screamed.

I slammed it shut. The elephant was in the passage! What is going on? Too nervous to sit down, I stood as far away from the shaking wall as possible and hoped that the elephant wouldn't knock it down. Nervous in the best of times, the elephant was now terrified and started to trumpet. I could hear the trainer trying to soothe him and quiet him down. Slowly, the din subsided until all was quiet. I cautiously opened the door and peeked out. All clear. I walked to the stage and asked the manager what had happened.

"What an idiot!" he fumed. "D'you know what the fool trainer did? He was late, so he brought the elephant through the stage door and tried to get him down this narrow passage. Well, he was too fat and he got stuck!"

"Where's the elephant now?"

"In the street, and it's raining! They had to back him out. Now, he'll have to wait until intermission when I can bring the curtain down and open the doors in the back."

I felt sorry for the elephant who not only had been traumatized but was probably going to come down with a cold. I went back to my dressing room, remembering not to get too close to the tigers' cages as I walked by.

As if two episodes in one week weren't enough, a third occurred involving our family. Sarah did an act with doves. Before each performance, an assistant placed some birds in cages off stage. Eleven others were placed in different parts of the theatre to be released at a signal. Sarah did several magic tricks where a dove appeared mysteriously out of a vase or a box. After about 10 minutes of awing her audience with the intelligence of her trained doves, it was time for Sarah's finale. Dressed from head to toe in white (probably so that the dove poo wouldn't show too much), Sarah stood on a platform, center stage, and raised both her arms to shoulder height. Suddenly, ten doves started flying around the auditorium. One by one, they landed on her – four on each arm, and two on her shoulders. Then, accompanied by a soft drum roll, a lone dove appeared. It circled several times over the audience before coming to rest on Sarah's turbaned head. It was a dramatic finish to her act. Sarah took her bow with all the pigeons, left the stage and started to walk up the stairs to her dressing room while still "wearing" all the birds.

As she passed my dad's dressing room, the door suddenly swung open and our bull dog Pancho ran out. At the sight of this vision in white, he started to bark. At this, all the birds took off.

"My birds! My birds!" screamed Sarah.

Everyone around tried to help, but not knowing how to go about it, we made things worse. Every time we got close to a bird, it flew off. In frustration, Sarah said, "I'll do it! Just keep still – all of you!"

We stood back and watched as she coaxed the doves back to her. By some miracle, they all responded, and she was able to get them back into their cages. After that, to avoid further confrontation with Pancho, she placed the birds in their cages the minute she came off stage.

Despite all the backstage traumas, this one-of-a-kind show was a success, but after four weeks Tom Arnold decided that the expense and multiple problems involved with moving large animals around the country was too much. I had enjoyed our time with the circus acts but was not going to miss having to step around the horse dung before going on stage for my tango or gagging at the stench as I passed the tigers' cages. Cats are clean animals, but because the cages were in such a confined area, the trainers were unable to hose out the cages daily as they normally did. I couldn't wait to go back to working in a theatre with people.

At the beginning of December, my dad informed me that on the 17th we'd be appearing in a pantomime for three weeks.

"It's going to be *Red Riding Hood* in Stockton-on-Tees," he said. "You know where that is – up north, about twenty miles from the east coast. In addition to the act, you'll all be taking different roles: Teddy (but billed as Raf) and Fe are playing Jimmy Green and Johnny Stout. You're Principal Girl, Marjorie Dawe."

"Oh, OK." I didn't think too much about it. It was a couple of weeks away, and I knew that in English pantomimes, Principal Girl was not quite like it sounds. The lead role is actually Principal Boy, which is played by a girl. The requirements for that role are: good legs (enhanced by short tunics, tights and high heels), an ability to deliver lines, and a commanding presence. A strong singing voice would be a plus.

My role, that of Prince Valiant's love interest, was less demanding. Mostly I was on a constant search, running on and off stage seeking either Red Riding Hood or Prince Valiant, and wondering where the big bad wolf was. I also had to stand and look adoringly at the Prince as he sang love songs to me. I found that if I focused my ardor on Garcia's eyebrows, I could give the situation all the ardor it required without laughing and messing up her solo.

Neither the management nor my dad had thought to tell me that I was supposed to have prepared two songs to sing. When the Musical Director asked me for my music, I just gaped at him in horror.

"I don't sing!" I blustered. "I mean I do sing, but my voice is thin. I do different stuff. I can't do two solos."

"Okay," he said." I guess we'll just have to do without."

Relieved, I thanked him and turned away, realizing I may be the only Principal Girl in English pantomimes who never sang a solo.

Chapter Twenty-Six

Shortly after breaking the news of our engagement to his family, Dick phoned me. He thought their reaction so funny that he had to tell me. From his sister-in-law, it was "Be careful and don't rush into things with that girl!" And his mother said, "There are lots of nice girls in America." And the stunner, "Just be sure she isn't after your money."

"Money! What money! How much do you have?"

"$8,000."

Well, that was a very nice nest egg but hardly a family fortune. I was hurt. We'd never even discussed money. Words just stuck in my throat. Finally, I said, "Well, as long as we are on the subject, I have a little money in the bank, too – 450 pounds. That's about $2,500. I'm really upset about this money thing."

"Oh, honey. Don't be. I'm the youngest in the family, and everybody thinks I'm still a kid. I thought it was funny."

"Well, I didn't."

"Don't worry about it."

I did worry about it but didn't want to take it out on Dick. It did make me wonder – what will his family think of me, this tap-dancing, piano-playing, Carmen Miranda impersonator?

My family didn't say much about my upcoming departure. They

said how much they'd miss me but not a word about how it would affect the act. My sister Fe, who would take my place, had just turned 16. She had different talents, did not play the piano but was a very good acrobat. There would have to be big changes. Only my Aunt Rosie expressed concern about my getting married. She said, "My dear, he has an open face, but you really don't know anything about him."

I shrugged and said, "Well, I love him. It'll be all right. You'll see."

Friends in show business were more outspoken.

"You're crazy! How can you give up show business? You have such a future! Aren't you going to miss the applause?"

I probably would. It had such a nice warm sound.

A future with Dick seemed much more exciting to me than one in show business. Older women in the theatre didn't look all that happy and contented. There was always a struggle to stay young-looking, and if there were children they usually ended up in boarding school. More than anything, I wanted a normal life.

Shortly after that call, Dick rang again. He said that some clothes he had sent back to California had arrived and that his mother was very happy.

"What do you mean? Why is she happy?"

"Well, as she unpacked my suitcase, she found the sweater you knitted for me. She said that any girl who could knit like that must be nice."

"What? Every girl in England knits like that. We learned in elementary school."

"Well, you've got to admit, it's funny."

There was another way of looking at it. If the day comes when I do miss the applause, I can always knit another sweater. I put my fears aside and told him about my news.

"Next month, we're going up to Scotland. There's going to be a special meeting in Edinburgh, and we've been invited. Why don't you see if you can come?"

"What's it all about?"

"Well, Edinburgh has always had festivals, which were suspended during the war. The city fathers want to revive them, have one every year. Now the war is over, and they can't wait to get started on their plans. It should be fun, and we'll meet a lot of interesting people. We're playing the Empire Theatre. I think that's why we're invited. And they do like our act."

"Well, as it's a month away, I might just be able to manage it."

"That would be wonderful!"

We were one of the few comedy acts that did well in Scotland. Most English comedians dreaded working there. Some even refused to go. It was a tough audience. If they didn't think you were funny, they'd let you know by whistling loudly. Nearly every English comic had a horror story about his engagement "up north."

We arrived in Edinburgh early on a Sunday morning and went straight to the hotel where the meeting was to be held. Many of the gentlemen who greeted us were in their full Scottish regalia, complete with kilt, sporran and a dirk stuck inside their argyle socks. There were many young girls, all dressed beautifully. Along with the kilts of their particular clan, they wore short, form-fitting black velvet jackets, set off with white, lacy blouses. At their throat were cairngorm brooches. The whole effect was elegant. The Scots were obviously proud of their heritage and wanted to express their pride on this important occasion.

Dick had managed to get a two-day pass from the Navy and walked in just as we were sitting down to lunch. The city fathers gave him a warm welcome, calling him "Laddie" and thrusting a tumbler-full of Scotch into his hand. Dick didn't drink and was a little dismayed but didn't want to insult his generous host by refusing. He took a sip every few minutes, but somehow the tumbler was forever full – someone kept filling it up.

After a delicious lunch, the mayor tapped his knife on a glass. When he had gained everyone's attention, he thanked them all for coming. He called on different men, introduced them to the group and asked them to explain what they had committed to do in order to get the Edinburgh Festival started up again. Little did any of us realize just how big and important the Festival would become and that some day it would be recognized as the biggest art festival in the world.

After numerous toasts, the atmosphere became very informal. Someone shouted, "Gie us a song, McGregor!" A tall gentleman stood up.

"I will if someone can play the piano," he said.

I waited to see if anyone else would volunteer. Nobody did, so I stuck my hand up. "I can. Do you have music?"

He just happened to have his music with him. We walked over to the piano. I sat down and put the music up. Luckily, I was a good sight reader and was not fazed by a cold reading. The song was "Roamin' in the Gloamin'." As I played the introduction, McGregor put his hand on my right shoulder. He had a good strong voice and we worked well together. Suddenly, his fingers dug into my shoulder. Ouch! I quickly realized that he wanted to hold that note and that I should stop playing until he was ready to continue. There were several more shoulder-pinchings as Mr. McGregor came well-prepared to the party and had brought lots of music. After six more songs, I begged off. My shoulder was killing me. I made the excuse that I had to leave to get ready for the show.

As the singing ended, so did the rest of the celebrations, and I went to look for Dick. I found him in a corner, swapping jokes with another happy gentleman. I don't think either one understood a word of what the other was saying.

"Man, these Scots really know how to drink," Dick said. "I've never had so much Scotch in my life!"

"Let's go back to the hotel," I said. "I've booked a room for you. I think we can all use a good night's sleep."

Nobody argued with that suggestion. We all walked to the hotel in various stages of sobriety, checked in and somehow got up to our rooms. It had been a happy and interesting day.

The next morning, I was excused from band rehearsal, so after getting my costumes and make-up put away in my dressing room, Dick and I took off to see the town. We'd both been there before, so we decided to stroll up and down Princes Street and window-shop. There wasn't much to buy – mostly kilts, which would have taken all my clothing coupons, and shortbread, the ever-popular Scottish delicacy.

"I'm hungry," Dick said. "Let's have lunch. I'm dying to try that haggis everyone talks about."

"Haggis! Do you know what it's made of?"

"No, all I know is that it's a traditional Scottish dish."

"Well, it's a mixture of the heart, liver and lungs of a sheep or calf, minced with suet, onions and seasonings. And if that isn't enough to turn you off, it's then boiled in the stomach of an animal."

"Sounds terrific. I'm game!"

"Well, I don't think we're going to find it in a restaurant. It's more of a home-made dish."

Dick was adventurous as far as food was concerned and willing to try anything. We hunted up and down Princes Street and all the little back alleys, but nowhere was haggis on the menu. I wasn't disappointed. We settled for some nice Scottish salmon.

"It's too bad we don't have time to visit Holyrood Castle and the Palace," said Dick. "I never get tired of looking at all that history, and it's so beautiful perched up there on the hill."

After lunch, we walked for three hours, and my feet were beginning to ache.

"I'll have to stop," I said, "or I won't be able to dance tonight. Maybe we can have a cup of tea somewhere and rest for a bit."

We found a little tea room which served some delicious scones along with our Twinings. And then it was time to go to the theatre.

We wouldn't go on until next to last, so Dick went off to chat with my dad while I put on my make-up. I thought it would be nice if Dick could see some of the show, so when I was ready I fetched Dick and took him downstairs to the stage. The stage manager gave permission for us to stand in the wings so long as we didn't get in anyone's way. Dick enjoyed watching performers from this different angle. He got a kick out of what they had to say after they took their bows. Sometimes it was about the audience – whether it was good or bad, or perhaps it was a rim shot the orchestra forgot. And sometimes it was about something their partner did wrong. It was always a tense moment.

We were watching the latest heart-throb singer from England, a good-looking man who sang dreamy love songs. After his second song, we became aware of some kind of disturbance in the audience. We didn't know what was happening. Suddenly, in a loud, clear, agonized voice, a woman screamed, "That's the man what ruined my daughter!"

A shock swept through the audience. The singer's jaw dropped, and he started to flap his arms up and down. The conductor played the introduction to the next song, but the singer's jaw kept going up and down without any sound coming out. Finally, he signaled the conductor to stop, grabbed the microphone and said, "Thank you, ladies and gentlemen. You've been a wonderful audience."

And with that, he left the stage. As he came off, he turned the air blue around him with every swear word he could think of.

"Let's get out of the way," I said to Dick. "The next act will have to go on."

The stage manager was irate. Ten minutes had suddenly been cut out of his program. "I'll talk to you later!" he shouted at the singer's back as he fled to his dressing room. "Mariora, are you ready to go on?"

Mariora was the juggler. She had been warming up backstage, ready to follow the singer. "Yes, I'm ready."

The stage manager phoned down to the conductor and told him of the change, and in a few seconds we heard Mariora's music.

Chapter Twenty-Six

"Phew!" I said to Dick. "I've never heard anything like that before. I don't think you're going to forget your trip to Scotland."

"You're right. That mother sounded so miserable. I wonder what's going to happen about her daughter. I hope that man does the right thing."

"Who knows? Well, the whole world knows about it now."

Dick's short trip to Scotland was over, and he had to return to base. As we said our goodbyes at the railway station, little did we know what news awaited him. He called immediately to tell me.

"The base is closing, and I'm being sent back to the U.S."

"Oh, my gosh! When?"

"As soon as I have destroyed all those airplane reports I've been so busy making in triplicate. That'll take a few weeks. I'm sure I'll get to see you before I go. By the way, what do you think of our getting married in New York?"

"New York! Why New York? We don't know anyone there! I want my family at the wedding. They can't go to New York!"

"OK, OK. We'll get married in Wimbledon. You make all the arrangements."

I was so wrapped up in the wish to be surrounded by relatives and friends for this big moment in my life that I didn't think about what I was asking of Dick. He would have to travel 7,000 miles for the big event. Nevertheless, he didn't complain. What I didn't know then, and what his mother told me later, was that the plan had been for her to go to New York for the wedding and then travel back to California with the two of us. I can't say I was disappointed for having missed spending the first two weeks of my married life as part of a threesome. Especially as the third person was my mother-in-law whom I'd never met.

Dick left in December. He went directly to San Diego where he would get a medical discharge. With his bad eye, the Navy should never have accepted him in the first place. He wrote to tell me that he was taking his mother to Palm Springs for a little vacation. They'd be there a week.

Chapter Twenty-Seven

We had four more weeks to do in Scotland. After Edinburgh, we went to the Empire Theatre in Glasgow. My mother had not been feeling well, so to give her a break we brought my little brother Richard and sister Juanita to Scotland with us. Our landladies in both cities were more than happy to baby-sit them while we worked, but on Sundays we spent all day with them.

On one of those Sundays, we were asked to do a show on an aircraft carrier. The ship was based near Edinburgh. It would only be possible if we could take Richard and Juanita with us. Permission was quickly granted. Someone decided that two small children did not constitute a threat to the Royal Navy. It was already dark at seven when we arrived at the docks at Queensferry just outside Edinburgh. There were no lights on anywhere, but a pale, thin moon shone a weak glow down on us. Sailors helped us board a small boat, and we started to motor quietly up the Firth of Forth. We passed the city of Rosyth, and as we drew nearer to our destination we began to see the outlines of several submarines. We all got very quiet. It was a surprise to all of us that a submarine base was so close to Edinburgh. The whole scene looked spooky and menacing in the moonlight. I'm glad they're on our side, I thought to myself.

It wasn't long before the aircraft carrier loomed into view, and we pulled alongside. One of the sailors picked Juanita up and hoisted her onto his shoulders. She was only four years old and getting sleepy. It was past her bedtime. Richard, who was ten, was excited and not about to miss anything. The rest of us followed and climbed the ladder to go aboard.

This was a huge ship, but quarters were very cramped. Some of the officers let us use their cabins as dressing rooms. We'd do the show in the officers' mess. It was a small room – the smallest space we'd ever worked in – and, of course, there was no stage. The "orchestra" of three pieces would have to squeeze into a corner.

After we'd made our quick tour of the premises, we found that Juanita had crawled up into a chair and fallen asleep. The captain looked at her and said, "Oh, she can't sleep like that. Follow me. She can sleep in my cabin."

I picked Juanita up and followed the captain to his quarters.

"Put her on my bunk. She'll be OK there."

"Oh, thank you so much. I really appreciate it."

"Not at all. I have two little girls of my own."

I left to get ready for the show, running back every few minutes to see how Juanita was. She was always sound asleep. We did the show but were embarrassed by what we thought was a poor performance. The confined space forced us to do several dance steps in place, and we constantly ran into each other as we made our entrances and exits through the only door. However, none of that seemed to bother the few officers who managed to squeeze into that little room.

They were most appreciative, but the experience was far different from the shows we did for ENSA where our audiences consisted of men from every level of the services. Never during the war did we do a show exclusively for officers. I could only think that they asked us because they were desperate to see fresh faces, and there was no other way to get civilians on board. The ship would soon be pulling out. The sailors and non-coms were on leave, but none of the officers was allowed ashore.

I went to wake Juanita to go back to our digs and was stunned to see a banana lying beside her. I hadn't seen a banana in five years.

"'Nita! 'Nita! Wake up! We have to go now. Look what the nice captain gave you."

She sat up rubbing her eyes.

"What is it?"

"It's a banana. You can eat it."

She picked it up, looked it over, then turned to me and said, "Will you take the cork out, Nena?"

New Year's Eve was coming up, and we had to move out of our digs. The landlady's rooms had been previously booked by someone else. We were able to get into the local hotel. This would be my first New Year's Eve in Scotland, and I really looked forward to it. For the Scots, it is the most important event of the year – bigger than Christmas. After the show, I couldn't wait to get back to the hotel to see what was happening. The lobby was filled with happy people, all drinking different types of cheer. It was 11:30, and there was a definite sense of anticipation in the air.

"What's going to happen at midnight?" I asked someone.

"Och, the drum major is coming with his bagpipes," the man answered.

I bought myself a glass of wine and searched for a vacant chair. It was fun watching the Scots having such a good time. At about two minutes to twelve, everyone suddenly got quiet. We could hear faint sounds of bagpipes in the distance. The music grew louder and louder, until at the stroke of midnight the drum major burst through the door. Larger than life, magnificent in full drum major regalia, complete with kilt and busby, he looked to be seven feet tall. He walked around the lobby, giving every individual full benefit of his bagpipes up close. It was deafening but exciting. After ten minutes, I left. Everyone was kissing someone, and I had no one to kiss. I went up to my room and fell into bed, happy that I'd finally experienced New Year's Eve in Scotland but wishing Dick could have shared it with me.

Chapter Twenty-Eight

There was a foregone conclusion in the family that Fe would go into show business. She was the only one of us who had attended a theatrical school. She studied many subjects, but the one thing she really wanted to learn – acrobatics, was not part of the curriculum. She begged my dad to teach her. He was reluctant saying there was no future in it. But Fe was determined and kept after him until she finally wore him down and he agreed.

They laid a tumbling mat out on the back lawn, and Dad erected a pulley contraption to facilitate the lesson. He was a good teacher, and Fe an eager student. It wasn't long before she had an impressive repertoire of acrobatic tricks. My dad was pleased with his student, and taught her a fast-paced routine ending with a row of back flips all across the stage. He decided to try her out in the act while I was still in it. He had a cute red bellboy costume made for her and suitable music written. The debut for this was to be at the London Palladium. This seemed to be the family's favorite theatre for debuts. Later, Chris Woodward, Archivist for the London Palladium, who had noticed the affinity between the theatre and our family, compiled a list of how often two or more Jovers had appeared at the theatre. Between the years 1913-1958 it was thirty-one times.

Her routine went over really well, but it threw the timing off in the act. This frustrated my dad who took it out on Fe who couldn't cope with his quick temper. Only sixteen years old and totally intimidated by him, she would burst into tears. This would elicit from him a scornful, "Sarah Bernhart!"

I had heard him call her that several times. I'd even seen him hit her, so I knew her fear of him was probably justified. Their relationship, or lack of it, was always a mystery to the rest of us.

I tried not to feel guilty over the situation. I could see stormy times ahead, but then I also felt entitled to lead the kind of life I wanted. I'd given nearly seven years to the act which was now well established. Now there were two brothers and a sister to help keep it going. Things were not as dire as in '39. I started to make plans for the wedding.

Dick thought he could make it back to England by the end of March. I selected Trinity Church in Wimbledon for the ceremony. The Banns would be read there for three consecutive Sundays prior to the event. After choosing the dates for that, I realized my wedding day would be on April 1. Hoping it wasn't an omen, I overcame my qualms and agreed to the dates. I then ordered a small reception at the Dog and Fox, a sort of glorified pub on Wimbledon Hill. Relatives generously donated their sugar and butter rations and our chickens their eggs for a traditional three-tier cake. Bakers would only make these cakes if you provided the ingredients. The next question was what to wear? There was virtually nothing decent available in England, even if I'd had the necessary clothing coupons. Dick solved that problem.

"Don't worry!" he wrote. "I'll bring you something. Send me your measurements."

Everything seemed to be falling into place. All I needed was my groom.

By law, after a sailor is discharged, the U.S. Navy is required to send him back to the place of enlistment. Dick's request to be sent back to Londonderry fell on deaf ears; it was too confusing for San Diego to cope with. He began his long trip first by train to New York, then ship to Southampton, then train to London and another to Wimbledon. He'd sent me a couple of cables on the way so that I could keep tabs on his journey. When he called from London to tell me when his train would arrive in Wimbledon, I was struck dumb thinking of how far he had come to marry me, and all I could think of to say was, "I'll meet you." He burst out laughing.

"Well, you'd better!" he said.

We had a wonderful reunion, and the family was happy to see Dick again. He'd been a hit with everyone. There was only a week to go before the wedding, but as it was to be a simple affair, there wasn't much left to do. Dick brought me a beautiful, pale blue wool suit that was a perfect fit. It was packed inside a new suitcase with my name engraved on it. I would be traveling in style. Shoes were a problem. I finally decided on a white, high-heeled pair I sometimes wore in the act. My hairdresser made a cute headdress of white netting and some flowers.

I was still working, so we dragged Dick off to the Finsbury Park Empire in London. I would take the following week off so that we could go down to Torquay on the south coast for our honeymoon. It was a lovely little wedding with only 15 guests. At one time during the ceremony, the young minister asked us to kneel. Two beautiful little velvet cushions had been provided for this purpose. Dick failed to see the cushions and sank down onto the hard, cold flagstones. I looked down at him and wondered what to do. Should I take advantage of that oh-so-comfortable-looking cushion or should I join Dick? I finally sank down onto those cold, hard flagstones also. The minister could hardly keep a straight face as he continued with the ceremony.

We all drove up to the Dog and Fox for the reception. There were the usual toasts and the cake-cutting. True to tradition, the top tier of the cake was put aside to be eaten on our first anniversary. We would mail it to California for his mother to save for us. It would keep well because it was a fruit cake covered with heavy, hard icing. Dick went into the kitchen and told the help that they could have the second tier. They couldn't believe his generosity. It was such a treat for them. I hoped that my aunts weren't too unhappy at seeing the sacrifice of their butter and sugar rations going to complete strangers. We took home what was left of the bottom layer.

Chapter Twenty-Nine

Dick and I were going to travel in the clothes we got married in, and as our packing was already done we grabbed a taxi and caught the train to Salisbury where we'd spend the first night. We stayed at the Red Lion Inn, a 12th-century coaching house. For years afterwards, we laughed about the five-foot-six doorways Dick kept banging his head on and the four-poster bed we slept in and had to prop up with pillows to prevent us from falling out onto the floor.

Torquay is a beautiful little town in Devon in an area often referred to as "England's Riviera." We had it practically to ourselves. April is usually a rainy month, but we were lucky and enjoyed sunshine all week. This part of the country had been spared the relentless bombing inflicted on London. We strolled through tiny villages just outside the town and marveled at the picturesque little cottages with thatched roofs. We even saw a man re-thatching a cottage. We were enthralled.

One day, Dick said, "Let's rent a rowboat and explore the harbor."

I warned him, "I'm not a good sailor."

"We're not going out to sea. It's just a rowboat."

I said, "All right," and hoped I wouldn't disgrace myself. We climbed into the boat, and Dick started to row. He rowed over toward the side of the bay where there were some caves. As we got closer to the ocean, the water was getting choppy, and my stomach queasy. I tried to will my breakfast to stay right where it was but finally had to say, "I think I'm going to throw up."

"Oh, no! We've hardly gone anywhere."

"I know. I'm sorry. Don't mind me. I'll just lie down."

"Oh, that's no fun. We'd better go back."

I felt terrible for having ruined our adventure in the harbor but was glad to be back on dry land. Although Dick was disappointed, he was understanding and didn't complain about my lack of seamanship. Before we knew it, our honeymoon was over, and we boarded the train for London. My agents, Lew and Leslie Grade, had given us two nights in a very nice hotel for a wedding present. We went straight there, calling the family to tell them we were back in town and that I'd be at Golders Green in time for the show.

After our two nights in the hotel, we moved in with the family in Wimbledon. Dick didn't seem to be in a big rush to go back to California. He wasn't sure what he wanted to do. He knew he didn't want to go to work for Lockheed again and even gave some thought to starting a business in the U.K. Frozen food was what he had in mind. He bought some books and read up on it but concluded England wasn't quite ready for that industry. Food was still not plentiful. Some of our short supplies were even going to Germany. They were in even more desperate need than England. Until things really came back to normal, the convenience of frozen food would have to wait.

Chapter Thirty

Our work was mostly around London and the south coast, and Dick enjoyed tagging along, soaking up more information about show business. We worked with another act that intrigued him.

It was called "Henry Vadden and Girls" and was a balancing act. The girls kept bringing different things to Henry for him to balance on his head. The items kept getting bigger and bigger. For his finale, the girls brought a beautiful dining table set for two. On the pink tablecloth were candles, glasses, silverware and even a vase of flowers. Everything was glued down, of course. The girls lifted the table up, and Henry attached a long pole to the underside of it. Then he slowly lifted up the pole with the table on it until he could rest it on a pad he had on his head. He walked slowly around the stage as the audience oohed and aahed at this amazing exhibition of strength. Suddenly, the music stopped, and there was a drum roll. With a crash of cymbals, Henry flipped the pole away and caught the falling table on his back. It was fortunate that he was facing upstage at this point as the look on his face and the swear words coming out of his mouth would surely have dampened the audience's enthusiastic applause.

"That guy's going to kill himself with that trick," Dick said. "What a way to make a living."

Four weeks went by, and we were back in Wimbledon. Raf was now home and out of the Royal Marines. He had completed his four-year service. Teddy understood the situation, and we all parted as friends. When things became more normal in Paris, France, he moved there and became a successful theatrical agent. We were supposed to work in Shepherd's Bush the following week, but I woke up Sunday morning with a terrible sore throat. Raf did, too. I couldn't eat anything, and the only thing I thought I could swallow was milk.

"Sorry," my mother said. "We only have enough for the little ones. How would you like some coffee?"

"Oh, no thanks. My throat hurts too much."

I couldn't eat or drink anything. Someone finally called the doctor. He looked at my throat and took a swab.

"My dear," he said. "We'll have to wait for the result of this test, but I think you have Diphtheria."

"Diphtheria! Nobody gets that anymore."

"Well, that's what it looks like to me, but we'll have to wait. It won't take long. You know, if the test results are positive, you'll have to go into isolation hospital."

"But I just got married!"

"Well, my dear, you have no choice. It's the law."

Things happened fast after that. The whole family and Dick were tested. Everyone else was negative, but Raf came up with a "maybe." The doctor re-tested him, and this time he passed. I was the only positive. Before I knew it, an ambulance arrived, and two men ran up the stairs with a stretcher. Dick was dismayed.

"Is this really necessary?" he asked the men.

"Oh, yes. With Diphtheria, the heart can get damaged easily in the early stages."

They wouldn't let him get anywhere near me, and all I could do was wave as I was whisked off to hospital.

The hospital, built at the turn of the century when Diphtheria epidemics were common, was not far from our house. I was wheeled into a 32-bed ward and was dismayed to discover I was the only patient. I was not allowed out of bed for anything. After some medication, it took only a couple of days for my throat to feel good. Not only that, a swab test came back negative.

"Can I go home now?" I asked.

"No, you have to stay the full six weeks. You tested positive once, so we have to watch your heart. And, as you're going to America, we have to be extra careful. The Americans are very particular about the health of immigrants."

I sank back onto the pillow. How will I ever survive six weeks in this place, I wondered. The nurses were kind and sympathetic, but there was nothing they could do to relieve my crushing boredom. Patients in other wards needed attention more than I, and so that's where they spent most of their time. The worst was at night when all the mice came out. They ran all over the place, including the nightstand next to my bed about a foot from my face. I had a horror of them climbing up onto my bed and crawling all over me. So much for protecting my heart – I was petrified. My pleas to the nurses fell on deaf ears. They just didn't want to take the mice out of the traps.

The few bright spots I had were the books Dick brought me to read and the notes he wrote. As the hospital was only a couple of miles from our house, he often rode my bike over there. Sometimes he brought me a treasure – an egg from our chickens. This always made the nurses nervous, as he couldn't resist drawing an ugly face on the egg and writing underneath "Matron."

"What if Matron sees this?" they gasped.

I hadn't had any problems with the Matron, but Dick was unhappy that she didn't allow him any kind of contact with me. Gradually, I was allowed some freedoms. The first was a 2-hour stretch, all bundled up in a wheelchair just outside the door to my ward. Then came the day when I could get dressed and walk around the grounds for 10 minutes. Dick got all excited.

"I know how we can at least see each other," he wrote.

"How can we do that?"

"I've done some exploring. There's a little building right by the fence. It's the morgue. When you go for your walk, slip behind the morgue, and I'll be on the other side of the fence. What time can you get there?"

"One o'clock. Right after lunch."

"It's a date. Tomorrow, one o'clock, behind the morgue."

We had one more week of trysts behind the morgue before the day arrived when I could finally go home. I felt like I'd been released from a long prison term. It was good to be home and back with Dick. He was now anxious to return to California. Six weeks with nothing to do and his wife in hospital helped him make up his mind. My new passport had arrived, and all that was left to do was pack and make travel arrangements.

Chapter Thirty-One

It was obvious my career in show business was over. During my six weeks' absence from the scene, my sister had to take my place in the act much sooner than anyone had anticipated. I didn't have any regrets about leaving show business and asked my dad how Fe was doing. He hesitated.

"Fine," he said. "She's doing fine."

Fe didn't look too happy, and I wondered how long it would be before she branched out on her own. She told me later that she only had two weeks to learn my part and complained that my costumes were old and didn't fit her.

I started to go through my stuff, trying to decide what to take and what to leave behind. Most of my clothes, I later found, were totally unsuitable for California. I couldn't find my best shoes – the ones I was married in.

"Has anyone seen my white shoes?" I kept asking.

Nobody answered, but they kept looking at Dick. Finally, he said, "Oh, I did something with them."

"What do you mean, you did something with them? What did you do?"

"I made them into platform shoes and painted them red. Fe's wearing them in the Carmen Miranda number."

"But those were my best shoes!"

I was furious, but bit my tongue as I reminded myself that Fe had no suitable shoes for the act. Also, I didn't want to have a fight with my husband in front of the family over a pair of shoes. I swallowed my anger and said, "Oh. That's all right then."

My only worry about leaving England was my mother. She had not been well but, typical of the day, did not share with her children what the problem was. No amount of begging on my part to see a doctor had any effect. When she finally did go, there wasn't much anyone could do. Perhaps she knew what was wrong and just didn't want to hear it. After leaving England, I never saw my mother again. She died of cancer later that year.

Dick booked passage out of Southhampton for August 19, 1946, on the *M.S. John Ericsson* of the United States Lines. We were told we could have only a small suitcase in our cabin. The rest had to go in the hold of the ship. I took my money out of the bank and bought traveler's checks. We planned to use them as we crossed the United States. I shipped a box of stuff off to California, wondering later whatever possessed me to spend good money sending such a load of junk that far. The only redeeming thing about it was the ammunition box I had packed everything in. Dick loved it and later used it to store tools.

Chapter Thirty-Two

At last, August 19th arrived, and the taxi drew up to the door. The whole family stood in the doorway to bid us goodbye. I was suddenly overcome with a terrible sense of loss and burst into tears. That set everyone off, and they all started crying. I wondered when, if ever, I'd see any of them again. I finally stopped sobbing and dried my eyes. We climbed into the taxi, waved our last goodbyes and drove to the station. Dick didn't say anything. He just held my hand. We caught the train to Southhampton and arrived an hour and a half later.

We had a short distance to walk to the boat. The *M.S. John Ericsson* looked like it had enjoyed better days. It still wore its battleship gray paint, having been used for troop deployment during the war. We could see that this was not to be a luxury cruise. The accommodations were basic. I was put into a cabin with seven other women, and Dick was in a cabin with about twenty men. Most of the passengers were war brides.

As the ship pulled away from the dock, I stood on the deck to savor my last view of England. It wasn't easy leaving my country. I was proud of my fellow Brits and how they had coped with the war, never complaining, making huge sacrifices, determined to beat the enemy at whatever the cost. And then there was my family – my parents and all my brothers and sisters. I knew I would miss them a lot. I gazed at the coastline until

Land's End, the most westerly point of England, came into view. It passed by and became just a tiny dot on the horizon. Then that too vanished, and all that was left was the ocean. It took our tired old ship nine days, two hours and fifty-nine minutes to cross the Atlantic. *The Queen Mary* off in the distance looked like a speed boat by comparison.

Dick and I would meet for breakfast, then spend the day together walking around the ship. There were no organized activities, but we got acquainted with other couples and passed the hours swapping stories about our hopes for the future. There was no privacy, but in the evenings as we strolled around we managed to find a few dark corners where we would snatch a kiss or two.

I thought that being on a big ship would take care of my queasy stomach, but three days out and I was flat on my back drinking tea with no milk and munching crackers. But a miracle happened, and after two more days I was fine.

The weather was gorgeous, and the sun beat down on us. Unfortunately, none of us on board was able to get to our luggage and dig out cooler clothes. The only time we could cool off was when we took our seawater showers.

The captain arranged a showing of a documentary for the war brides. It was a sort of get-acquainted travelogue of America. The girl sitting next to me said she was going to "Canarycut." She dug me in the ribs when the tiny Glendale Grand Central Airport suddenly appeared on the screen. It was startling to see an actual picture of my destination.

As we neared New York, passengers crowded the deck. A lady who spoke no English took my hand, walked me over to the rail and pointed. It was the Statue of Liberty. She turned to me with tears in her eyes and a big smile on her face. Being suddenly up close to this world-famous symbol of freedom was breathtaking. I swallowed a big lump in my throat, smiled back at the lady and squeezed her hand. We couldn't communicate verbally, but there really was no need for words.

Chapter Thirty-Three

We arrived in New York on a Sunday. No teamsters were working, so we stayed in the harbor overnight. But the Immigration officer did come aboard to record our entry. We could clearly hear the traffic noise from the streets and were very close to all those gigantic skyscrapers I'd heard so much about. I couldn't imagine what it would be like to work in an office so high up in the sky.

The next morning, we disembarked and took a taxi to a hotel. It was hot and humid. I had never experienced such heat. How are people able to live in this climate, I wondered. Some of them are actually running!

We had a room on the eighth floor. The fresh water showers were heavenly. However, by the time I took the elevator down to the ground and went out into the street, I needed another shower. We walked around New York, and I was astounded at the energy everyone seemed to have. They all looked like they were in a hurry. I wondered what they were all rushing to that was so important.

We went into a café for lunch. It was air conditioned and so comfortable. I was totally overwhelmed by the menu, never having seen such a variety of choices. Dick suggested the cantaloupe, which I'd never had before. Half a cantaloupe arrived, the center filled with ice cream. It was so cold; it put my teeth on edge. Nothing in England was ever served that cold. I found that by letting the cantaloupe sit on my tongue for a few seconds, it would warm up, and I could eat it. It was delicious.

When we got back to the hotel, there was something I had to tell Dick. I'd kept it to myself too long and had been waiting for just the right moment. I didn't know how he'd take the news. I blurted out, "I think I'm pregnant."

"Are you sure?"

"Well, my period is two weeks late, and I'm never late."

"Well, it's sooner than we planned," he said with a grin. "It will complicate things, but we'll manage."

It was such a relief to know that Dick was not worried over my news. We didn't have a place to live, he didn't have a job, and now there were to be three of us. But he had a positive outlook on life and was confident everything would work out just fine. I had my qualms. Will I be able to cope with all the radical changes taking place so suddenly in my life?

"I think we should take the train to Detroit and buy a car," Dick said. "We'll drive across the country. That'll give you a chance to see America."

"Sounds like a wonderful idea."

We took the night train, saving one more night in an expensive hotel. But we were in for a shock. There were no new cars available in Detroit as the factories had not yet converted from tanks to cars. We finally settled on a used Buick. It was a "blackout model," so-called because there was no chrome on it. Rather than go through the red tape of getting Dick's money from the bank in California, we decided to use my traveler's checks. We had not planned well for this; the car cost $1,200, and my checks were all in small denominations. I sat at the desk for what seemed like hours signing check after check. Finally, the deed was done, and the car was ours. We threw our belongings into the trunk and took off.

Dick wanted to avoid the worst heat, so he decided we'd take the northern route to California. He would have to do all the driving. Even though I took driving lessons in the U.K., I never did get my license. I knew all about double de-clutching, etc., but as my dad only let my brothers drive our big Wolseley, there was no real incentive for me to get that license. I saw that everyone in America seemed to be driving on the wrong side of the road anyway, and I was in no rush to join them.

We left Detroit and soon entered the rural area of Michigan. I went into raptures over how beautiful the pristine lakes and trees were. Dick, who grew up in Southern California and was a sun worshipper, was not impressed. "You should see their winters – they're miserable."

We drove briefly through the northern parts of Indiana and Illinois. To help pass the time, we turned on the radio and tuned into the news. The announcer solemnly gave the statistics on how many people were currently suffering from Infantile Paralysis (Polio).

This terrible disease was not a problem in England and had not got a lot of attention there, but as we drove across the States the daily updates of new cases grew. There didn't seem to be much hope for a cure. Most sufferers had to live in what the announcer called an "iron lung." It sounded like a fate worse than death.

Suddenly, we were in Iowa.

"Gosh! Look at all that corn!" I said.

Accustomed to the small fields of crops in England, the sight of miles and miles of corn was staggering. I understood then why the U.S. was able to send so much of it overseas.

"We should get some good corn when we stop for dinner," Dick said.

But it was not to be. Corn wasn't even on the menu. We concluded the locals must be so sick of the sight of it that the thought of eating it was too much.

Every day, we bought stuff for lunch and then looked for a tree to sit under to eat it. When we entered Nebraska, that was a problem. There were very few trees. One day, we drove for miles with no tree in sight. Suddenly, I saw one on the horizon.

"There's one!" I shouted.

We were both hungry and couldn't wait to reach it. Even though we could see it, it was still miles away. Finally, we arrived. We got out of the car, picked up our lunch and walked over to the tree. Our hearts sank. Seven cows and thousands of flies had already claimed ownership. We were crushed.

"There's gotta be another tree in Nebraska," Dick said, as we got back into the car. We went on for a few miles, but there was not a single tree. We gave up the search, stopped in the middle of nowhere and quietly ate our lunch.

"Did you know we're in the middle of the 48 states?" Dick said.

"D'you mean we've been driving for five days, and we're only halfway there?"

"Afraid so. Getting tired?"

"No, but I can't believe after all this driving we're still in America."

It felt like we were going to the ends of the earth. It was not like Europe where you could drive through three or four countries in one day.

Nebraska was sparsely populated, and there was a shortage of accommodations for travelers. We usually stayed in small, almost primitive, motels, but one night after hours of driving we found nothing. In desperation, Dick went to the police station in a tiny little town and told a police officer of our predicament. Lucky for us, he had a solution. He telephoned a lady who told him to send us to her house right away. She made us welcome, fixing us dinner and providing us with a clean, comfortable bed. In the morning, we had a wonderful breakfast to send us on our way. This lady was so warm. I appreciated her kindness as I was now experiencing morning sickness and didn't feel so great. We insisted on paying her even though she was reluctant to take anything.

As we crossed the border into Wyoming, Dick said, "We're going to go through Yellowstone National Park. This is a first for me too."

We pulled up to the entrance where the ranger welcomed us with a smile, handing me a brochure and a map. I could see that this park was not like parks in England. The immediate impression was of ruggedness on a grand scale. I opened the brochure and started reading all the statistics.

"Don't read that now," said Dick. "Let's just look. We can read all that later. Why are all those cars stopped up ahead?"

We slowed down to see what had interested everyone. It was bears! They were just off the road. People were throwing out peanuts and loaves of bread. The bears ambled across, picking up and eating whatever they fancied. I couldn't understand this.

"Isn't this dangerous? The only bears I've ever seen were in zoos behind strong bars."

"Oh, they won't bother you. Stand outside the car, and I'll take your picture."

I was terrified and didn't want to do that but thought, "This is Dick's country. He must know what he's doing." I got out of the car, but kept one hand on the door handle. The bear was lying down in the middle of the road barely six feet from me. As soon as I heard the camera click, I was inside like a shot. Dick laughed, but many years later I felt vindicated when all the national parks started to prohibit the feeding of bears.

We drove on, getting out of the car once in a while to walk over to a fumarole or mud pot. Unfortunately, a mere whiff of the nauseous gases coming from them was all that was needed to arouse my morning sickness. It was a relief to stand in front of Old Faithful and watch it spout water a hundred feet into the air. There were more surprises – large herds of bison and elk. We could have spent days in the park. There was so much to see, but we finally left and looked for a place to eat dinner.

As we pulled into a restaurant, Dick said, "This is cattle country. We should order steak."

When it arrived, my jaw dropped. It was on a platter and was so large it hung over the edges. It looked like a week's ration for a British family. I couldn't help but think of my family and how they would enjoy such a feast. I started to say, "How in the world can two of us eat all this?" when a similar steak was placed in front of Dick. I gasped and threw up my hands. There was no way I could do justice to mine. Dick, who loved meat, eyed my uneaten portion and asked the waitress if we could take the rest of my steak with us. She was a little taken aback but obliged by wrapping it up in some paper. I was embarrassed. I'd never heard of anyone taking food out of a restaurant but was happy it wasn't going to waste.

We got back on the road, passing through the northern part of Utah and into Nevada and the Mojave Desert. The heat was almost more than I could cope with. It was really getting to me. Our car, of course, had no air conditioning. As we drove through the desert, I gazed with longing at billboards with their enticing ads of ice-cold cans of beer.

"Oh, that looks so good. Can we stop and get a beer?"

"It'll cost an arm and a leg, and you'll only feel cool for a few minutes. We're better off drinking water."

"Oh."

He was probably right, but I couldn't get the picture of those ice-cold cans out of my head. I'd never drunk beer before, mostly because my dad didn't like to see women drinking beer. "It looks so unladylike," he would say.

We drove south to Las Vegas, parked the car and walked in and out of several casinos. It was an amazing sight – dozens of people with grim looks on their faces, sitting in front of rows of slot machines. We squandered a few nickels, then went back to the car. Perspiration was just dripping off us, and the car was like an oven.

"This road is called 'The Strip,'" Dick said. "There's another casino down there."

We started to drive down this straight road. In the distance were two tall buildings. They looked so forlorn, surrounded by nothing but desert. As we got nearer to them, I could see that one was called "Thunderbird" and the other "The Flamingo."

"That one was built just this year by a gangster, Bugsy Siegel," Dick said.

I looked at this elaborate building with cement pink flamingos by the entrance and couldn't wait to go inside. A pall of blue cigarette smoke hung over a large room. Underfoot was thick carpeting, and overhead elaborate chandeliers. Apart from rows of slot machines, there were several tables where people were playing some sort of card game. Pretty girls in skimpy costumes carrying drinks wandered from table to table. I felt like I'd been dropped into another world. My mind flashed back to the casinos my dad had performed in on the French Riviera – so quiet and dignified, the guests mostly royalty and titled people. The Flamingo was noisy, glitzy and more democratic in its clientele. This was not Dick's favorite milieu, and we were soon on the road again.

"We're not far from California now," said Dick. "Just a few hours."

Shortly after we crossed the border, we passed several fruit stands. Dick pulled over to one of them.

"You're about to have your first California peach."

I couldn't believe how big, sweet and juicy it was. The juice ran down my arms and dripped off my elbows.

"Oh, my gosh! I've never tasted anything like this! When I think of those awful things we bought in England!"

We never bought peaches for ourselves, but if we had a friend in hospital we bought a hot-house grown peach as a special treat. It was expensive, small and hard as a rock. The patient would probably never be able to eat it but would be comforted knowing that you cared enough to spend your money on such a luxury item for him.

"Look!" Dick said.

It was a "Welcome to Glendale" sign.

"Oh, we're finally here. It's beautiful."

Nestled at the base of the mountains, Glendale with its clean, orderly streets looked peaceful and friendly. "How lucky I am," I thought.

I would have gone anywhere with Dick, but this place looked like heaven. Along with my pleasant surprise came feelings of hope, fear and trepidation. My head was full of questions. "Will his family like me? Will I like them? Where will we live? What will Dick do to make a living?" Will I have a boy or a girl?"

As we drove through the streets to his mother's apartment, my heart started to pound. I realized how different my life would be from this day on. I was no longer a dancer/singer/piano player, flitting from town to town every week. Now, I was a wife, soon to be a mother and probably destined to stay in this city for the rest of my days. The journey to California, filled with fun and excitement, was over, and I could only guess what the journey ahead held for me. But I was confident. Hadn't I proved to myself that I was up to any challenge? Hadn't I survived the war with its relentless bombing and even sung in Portuguese at the London Palladium? Dick stopped the car and turned off the ignition. I took a deep breath and got out.

Epilogue

After my mother died, my dad married Pat Cox, a dancer. They had two children. Variety was declining in popularity. Many theatres closed to become bingo parlors, and work was scarce. Dad left show business and became a travel guide with Global Tours. His marriage didn't last, and after the divorce, he lived for a while in Torremolinos, Spain, then immigrated to America and died at 86 in Tujunga, California.

After leaving the services, Raf and Julian joined forces and created a new act. It was successful with appearances on the Ed Sullivan TV show, at the London Palladium, and in various spectaculars. It ended when Julian married Australian radio star, Kitty Bluett and they left with their daughter, for Australia. He entered the TV industry and rose to Executive Producer for Channel 7 in Sidney. Today, he lives in Bundaberg with his second wife, Lyn. Deciding to leave show business and start a new life, Raf left England for California with his wife and daughter, where he started a car insurance business. Today, he lives in Hollywood, with his life companion, Bernice.

After his service in the Royal Air Force, Richard went back to his job at Lew and Leslie Grade's theatrical agency. In 1957 he accepted our invitation and joined us in California. Shortly after, he married Jeanne

Phillips. He went back to school and became a Customer Engineer with IBM. After Jeanne died, Richard married Patricia Scardino in 1978.

Variety was in its last throes when Juanita graduated from Catholic school in Wimbledon. She held various jobs before marrying Lewis Benjamin. They had two sons. She lost her battle with cancer and died at 42.

Fe is the only Jover sibling to have had an extensive career as a performer. It was highly successful and lasted over sixty years. After two years with our dad, she struck out on her own. After she met and married Wilfred Halliwell, an equilibrist, they formed a comedy act, "The Jovers," touring Europe and the Middle East. They came to America in 1963, and toured for two seasons with the Harlem Globe Trotters. Following that were four appearances on the Ed Sulllivan TV show, two years touring with Liberace, and twenty years in numerous extravaganzas in Las Vegas. They came out of retirement for two seasons in The Palm Springs Follies. Today, Fe and Wilf live in Show Low, Arizona.

Dick and I settled in Glendale, California and raised three children. In the early 1950s, Dick developed a revolutionary-designed backpack. He cut, shaped, and welded aluminum frames in the garage while I sewed nylon bags to be attached, in the kitchen. Richard also helped doing various jobs. Word soon spread to eager adventurers from Mount Everest expeditions and ordinary people wanting a comfortable backpack. Convinced there was a market for our product, we borrowed $400 and set up shop. Today, KELTY is a world-wide multi million dollar enterprise. Dick died in 2004 at the age of 84.

After five generations in the entertainment business, the family's name has disappeared from all theatrical programs. Perhaps one of our many offspring will take up the baton and continue what was started so long ago in Spain.

www.ingramcontent.com/pod-product-compliance
Lightning Source LLC
Chambersburg PA
CBHW071229170426
43191CB00032B/1139